The Vegetarian Lunchbasket

The Vegetarian Lunchbasket

Over 225 EASY, Lowfat, Nutritious, RECIPES
for the Quality-Conscious Family ON THE GO

LINDA HAYNES

NEW WORLD LIBRARY
NOVATO, CALIFORNIA

New World Library
14 Pamaron Way
Novato, CA 94949

© 1990, 1994, 1999, Linda Haynes

Cover art and design: Kathy Warinner
Spot art in chapter openers: Kathy Warinner
Interior how-to art: Haven Haynes Leask
Revised edition editing: Gina Misiroglu
Text design and layout: Tona Pearce Myers
Indexing: Alta Indexing Services

Library of Congress Cataloging-in-Publication Data

Haynes, Linda, 1951-
    Vegetarian lunchbasket: over 225 easy, lowfat, nutritious recipes for the quality conscious family on the go / written by Linda Haynes. — Rev. ed. / edited by Gina Misiroglu.
        p.   cm.
    ISBN 1-57731-087-X (alk. paper)
    1. Vegetarian cookery. 2. Luncheons. 3. Lunchbox cookery.
I. Misiroglu, Gina Renée. II. Title.

TX837.H394 1999
641.5'636—dc21   99-23544
                                                                          CIP

First Revised Printing, September 1999
ISBN: 1-57731-087-X
Printed in Canada on acid-free paper
Distributed by Publishers Group West

10 9 8 7 6 5 4 3 2 1

For my small and large family

Contents

Preface

The original *Vegetarian Lunchbasket* was written when my family was younger, with higher metabolisms. These days, we are all a little more careful in our eating habits. The girls are watching their fat intake for their bodies and skin, and our youngest is the fastest man on the soccer field as long as he is eating well.

You may notice that recipes often call for flour without specifying what kind. I have left that up to your conscience and taste. Whole-wheat is heavier and healthier than unbleached. It gives a heartier, rougher taste to foods. If you do not eat wheat, use rice, oat flour, or barley flour for thickening. If you do not eat dairy products, replace them with soy milk, nut milk, oat milk, or rice milk. As to fats, there are many opinions. Some people do not tolerate dairy fats, some find certain oils indigestible. I have suggested what I think tastes best, but the choice is up to you.

I have added the lower-fat alternatives that I often use. Essential fatty acids are important to good health, and children's nervous systems, especially, need them, but heating fats changes their nature, and fats seem to carry many chemical contaminants, so using good organic oils is best.

Serving sizes have been indicated on most recipes. However, serving size is a very relative term. If you have a picnic of sandwiches, a pasta salad, a green salad, vegetable chips and dip, and a cake, then your helping of green salad would probably be much smaller than a luncheon of only a green salad and bread sticks. Most serving sizes have been calculated assuming that the dish would be part of a two- to three-item meal. So, take the calculations with a grain of salt, so speak, and enjoy your meal!

I have also added many new recipes. In the years since this book was first published, our family has continued to experiment and play with foods. Many Asian foods and spices are more widely available. Supermarkets now carry fresh herbs, and farmer's markets and organic food chains, such as Whole Earth or other natural food co-ops, are abundant across the country. Partly due to these trends, and partly due to good role models, children today are more adventurous in their eating habits. Adults, too, are interested in eating foods rich in enzymes and vital forces. With all of these changes, it was time for a new edition.

My hope is that you will enjoy the new recipes, and experiment a bit on your own. Whether you are vegetarian or someone who wants to start incorporating more vegetables, fruits, and grains into his or her diet, this book has something for everyone.

Introduction

When I first became a vegetarian, the only things I knew how to cook were frozen vegetables and macaroni and cheese. Gradually, I learned how to make bean stews and grain casseroles. Through the years, my kitchen ways have changed with the new foods or ideas I have discovered. My experiments turned the kitchen into a laboratory. Well remembered are the year of the soybean, the month of agar gels, and Sunday-night gluten dinners. The happy result of this experimenting is a basic knowledge of the various ingredients, and hence my style of cooking: alchemy!

After I have tried a recipe I rarely use it again except as a reference for certain proportions, such as baking powder-to-flour ratio. I personalize it by excluding items that my family doesn't eat. I include spices, add to the protein content, use leftovers, or take advantage of a bumper crop from the garden. Please do the same with the recipes in this book. Have fun with cooking; let it nurture your creativity as well as the health of those you love.

Vegetarian Lunches on the Run

When my children started school, we were caught unprepared for packing lunch boxes. I didn't mind going to work with a baked squash under one arm, but little ones are subject to teasing and peer pressure. Even my husband was tired of squash on or off the cuff. The answer seemed to be sandwiches, but someone wouldn't eat bread and someone else said whole grains were hard to digest at a sit-down job. We began experimenting, asking friends, and thinking creatively to come up with new ideas. The results — packable, tasty, easy, healthful, reasonable-looking vegetarian lunches — I'm happy to share with you here.

Fast Foods and Do-Aheads

The best way to save time in the kitchen is to be organized. It really works. I used to make a large batch of soup base, put it into ice cube trays, transfer it to plastic bags in the freezer and then forget about it. A few months later, I'd find these brown-flecked cubes and I'd think that something had gone rotten. One day at my grandfather's house, I noticed a list on his freezer door. Frozen foods were listed under their categories, along with a shelf number and date of entry. I went home and organized the freezer and the pantry, too. Things rarely get lost now. Organization allows the cook to shop less and to move quickly in the kitchen. Making food in large batches, storing, and portioning it saves trips to the garbage cans and compost pile.

Many recipes can be doubled and half of the dish frozen for another time. This is good to do with beans, especially chickpeas (garbanzo beans) which are hardy little guys. Potatoes are grainy after freezing and no one likes them much. Fruit in season is cheaper and tastes better; freeze it for use out of season. In season is a good time to can, or freeze, or to make dry batches of fruit leather, conserves, chutneys, and sauces. Put things up in small containers and avoid waste; anything not eaten the first day after opening seems to go into an "untouchable" class.

Sometimes I keep bags of roasted soy flour (called *kinogoshi*), chickpea flour, or dry burger mix in the refrigerator to preserve their nutrients and keep them fresh. Toasting and roasting seeds, nuts, and soybeans can be done once a week in a few minutes, as can sprouting, making yogurt, and with more time, bread baking. Some people can do all this once a week; I rotate, doing one for a few weeks, then another. Having the kitchen and foods in order does save time.

When I get up in the morning, I don't expect to prepare gourmet lunchbaskets from scratch. Rather, I assemble lunches while amusing the baby in his high chair, looking for lost socks, and putting out breakfast possibilities. Most of us do experience a morning time crunch; having readily available ingredients made ahead is important when you want to provide more than peanut butter-and-jelly on the run.

Leftovers

When I cook supper, I think about lunches for the next day and design the meal so that I can use its components for lunches. For example, Split Pea Soup is a good supper if we've been out skating, and in the morning I heat it up for lunch thermoses. Sometimes someone will want it for breakfast, too. Even if supper is just a salad, I make it big enough so that the next morning it can be thrown in a pot and simmered with broth or tomato sauce. Voilà! Minestrone soup, in the time it takes to braid two heads of hair. Many of the recipes here use leftovers.

About Preheating the Oven

For ecological reasons, I rarely preheat the oven except when baking breads, desserts, or dishes that have a short baking time. The recipes will still work if cooked in a pre-heated oven.

About Packaging

I packed lunches in empty yogurt and cottage cheese containers until one day I noticed how inelegant and unappetizing it looked. I started thinking about how airlines handle moveable meals (all those little dishes), and decided that a horizontal lunch looked better than a vertical one. Now I use low flat covered plastic boxes (like Tupperware). Horizontal also lets you choose the order in which to eat your food. This was a major breakthrough. The next obvious step is the palette effect. A dab of cranberry sauce brightens up fried tofu, and several pale green leaves from last night's artichokes look nice next to a few black olives.

A spoonful of toasted sesame seeds sprinkled over a lunch freshens it up. A tablespoon of chutney is a nice flavor in juxtaposition to curried rice and vegetables. Carrot sticks add some color and raw crunch to a lunch of burger and applesauce. Somehow an impromptu salad appears, and leftovers get used before they hit the slimy oblivion at the back of the refrigerator. Lunch has flavor, colors, textures, and variety, all of which gets the digestive juices going.

Children enjoy separate little packages (have you ever seen what happens to lunch boxes in the cloak room?). Kept separate, the food won't get soggy or discolored. Dipping into little, plastic, Tupperware-type containers is fun, and small packages are tradable.

We tried discouraging trading, but settled for a lecture on nutrition and hoped for the best. Our daughter took toasted sunflower seeds, peanuts, and fruit leather to school every day for months. I found out later that she was trading with everyone at her table for their carrots (she wanted to be able to see in the dark). This year, she started asking for corn chips every day. When confronted with their dubious nutritional value, she explained, "Oh, I don't eat them, but Gretchen's mother sends her with the most delicious plums." We decided that trading isn't so bad.

Sometimes I buy packaged items such as a case of little bottled juices, a box of fruit leathers, or applesauce in baby food jars (take off the labels to prevent teasing) to save some time. Bought in large quantities, they can be economical.

Your choice of containers may be dependent upon your resources. For example, you may need to consider if you can fit your lunch into the tiny office refrigerator, whether you'll be heating it up in a microwave or conventional oven, and if you can afford to occasionally lose a plastic container to the school lunchroom.

Ingredient Glossary

You may be unfamiliar with some of the items called for in these recipes. Don't let that stop you; substitute, or better yet, get to know how to use these healthy, delicious alternatives. Where possible, I have listed mail-order sources in the back of the book.

Adzuki beans: A small red bean, often sweetened and used as a paste in Japanese or Chinese sweets.

Agar agar, or kuzu: A seaweed, often sold in powder form, that forms a jell-like food. It's tasteless by itself but takes on the flavor of other ingredients.

Aromatic bean curd: Also called dried aromatic bean curd, pressed tofu, or savory tofu. All of them are sold in Asian markets in 4 oz. cakes sealed in plastic. They are easily sliced or slivered, and they are very high in protein.

Arrowroot: A natural thickener that can be used like cornstarch or tapioca flour.

Bean thread (cellophane) noodles: These are a type of vermicelli that turn transparent when cooked. They are made from bean gelatin, usually from mung beans.

Chapatis: Flat, unleavened breads, homemade or found at an Indian grocery or natural foods store.

Chili oil: Hot! Available in Asian markets.

Dried chestnuts: Sold in packages in Asian markets, these should be soaked for several hours before cooking.

Dried tofu skins or yuba: Not technically a tofu, *yuba* is the skin that forms on the top of heated soy milk. It is sometimes sold fresh or frozen in plastic packages, and often it is dried either in big flat sheets or in long twisted strings. It is best to soak this dried form several hours before cooking. This tofu is the highest vegetarian source of protein known.

Dried vegetable flakes: These are little chips of dried vegetables that can be home-made or are available ready-made in the spice section of a supermarket (next to dried onion flakes).

Dried vegetable flour: These can be purchased through King Arthur Baking Company or produced at home by dehydrating sliced vegetables and grinding them into a powder.

Dulse: This is an edible seaweed. It is a good source of calcium, magnesium, potassium, iron, and of course iodine. It is available dried in packages in Asian markets.

Filo (phyllo): A pastry dough that is extremely thin and layered (this is what the Greek pastry baklava is made with). It's difficult and time-consuming to make, but can be purchased in the grocery freezer section. Thoroughly defrost before using.

Fresh ginger — or ginger root: This is a bulbous-looking rhizome. It is available in most grocery stores. It really isn't very interchangeable with the dried powder, which tastes dead in comparison. The root is usually grated or sliced very fine. Look for plump roots as the roots get dry and woody as they start to age or sprout.

Gluten flour: The protein part of wheat, free of starch and bran. Gluten, also called *seitan*, which is made from this flour, is often used as a meatlike substitute and can be purchased in the refrigerated case at natural foods stores.

Glutinous rice: This rice cooks up to be very sticky, almost like tapioca. It is used to make *mochi* (sticky little cakes often sweetened or dipped in sweet sauce). Available in Asian markets or the foreign foods section at the grocery.

Goma-shio: Available in health-food stores and some Asian markets, *goma-shio* is a seasoning composed of sea salt and toasted sesame seeds.

Hing: Also called *asafetida*. A dried resin from the ferul plant (related to fennel). It is commonly used in East Indian cooking as a substitute for onion and/or garlic. It has a powerful, noxious smell when raw. The taste in cooked food resembles shallot or garlic. Use the yellow Cobra brand found in Indian or Middle Eastern grocery stores, or supermarkets with international foods sections. One small container lasts for months. I keep it in the garage to keep the odor out of the kitchen.

Lavash: A Middle Eastern wheat flat bread. Available at Middle Eastern groceries or in the international foods section of some large supermarkets.

Millers bran or wheat bran: Is made from the outer coating of wheat (often removed when producing white flour). It is an excellent source of fiber. Keep it in the refrigerator or freezer to prevent rancidity.

Miso: A fermented soybean paste, high in protein, helpful bacteria, and B vitamins, used as a seasoning. Dissolve it first in a small amount of hot water; do not boil. Available at natural foods stores or Asian markets. There are many kinds of miso. Some are made of soybeans and others are made of soybeans combined with other beans or grains. Each kind has its own flavor. I find the white or yellow to be the mildest tasting.

Mung beans: Look like tiny dried peas the size of bb's. They are often made into dahl or Indian cuisine and are easily sprouted to make the bean sprouts used in Asian cuisine.

Nori: A seaweed that comes in flat sheets. Can be purchased at natural foods stores or Asian markets.

Nutritional yeast: Yellow flakes that are very high in B vitamins. Nutritional yeast is different from brewer's yeast (which has a different look also: brownish granules); the latter has a bitter taste. Can be purchased at natural foods stores. It is mild and almost cheesy. My children sprinkle it on almost everything

Pastry flour: This flour is made from wheat with a lower gluten or protein content. A high gluten flour is important in bread baking as it has great elasticity, but it would make tougher, chewier cakes and pastries.

Pickled ginger: Sold in packages or jars in Asian markets, pickled ginger is made by pickling slices of ginger root in sugar and vinegar. Often eaten as a sushi condiment.

Pita bread: Flat, round unleavened bread. When you cut it in half, you get two "pockets." Can be purchased at your local grocery.

Rice paper wrappers: Thin flour wafers; available in Asian markets in the refrigerator or freezer section, or in the produce section of your supermarket.

Sesame oil: Is expressed from toasted sesame seeds and has a rich unique flavor.

Soy flour: Is made from ground soybeans. Roasted or toasted soy flour is made from ground roasted soybeans. It has no gluten in it, so while it will boost protein in baked goods, it will make them a little more dense.

Soy grit: Are made of soybeans that have been chopped up (but not so fine as meal or flour). They often have been pre-soaked and dried. They require much less cooking time than ordinary soybeans. Available in natural foods stores.

Tahini: A paste made from crushed sesame seeds. It's a good binder and has a creamy, nutty flavor. It is smoother and more flowing than sesame butter, so it's not a good idea to substitute. Can be purchased at natural foods stores.

Tamari sauce: An aged soy sauce made from soybeans, salt, and water. Some are made with wheat, some are wheat free. It has a richer taste than regular soy sauce. Can be purchased at natural foods stores, Asian markets, or in the international foods section of your supermarket.

Texturized vegetable protein (TVP): Is made of soy flour that has been extruded, pressed, or heated. When used in cooking, it has the texture of ground meat. Available through co-ops or natural foods stores.

Tofu: A soy food made from curdling soybean milk and pressing the curds into cakes. Tofu is a high-protein food that is bland in taste but can be added to recipes, fried, and spiced. It should be kept in the refrigerator in a tub of water for up to two weeks. Used in recipes, it can be left at room temperature for several hours. It can be purchased in the produce section of most supermarkets, at natural foods stores, or Asian markets. Different styles are available; generally, soft or silken tofu is good for sauces and blending, while firm tofu is better for frying. Silken tofu is a custard-like tofu that breaks apart easily and has a very mild flavor. I usually just buy extra-firm tofu and use it for everything (it blends up very smooth).

Umoboshi plums: Taste a little sour and very salty. They are made by pickling unripe little plums in salt. They are an aid to digestion, and we use them at our house to cure stomach aches. They are sometimes made into a paste. Available at Asian markets or the foreign foods section of the grocery.

Vegetable broth or vegetable stock: Is the nutritious and flavorful water in which vegetables have been simmered.

Wasabi powder: Powdered Japanese horseradish root; available in Asian groceries.

White-wheat flour: This is a type of whole-wheat flour that is naturally white and lighter than regular whole-wheat. Available from King Arthur Baking Company, and I've even seen it on grocery shelves.

CHAPTER I

Breads, Wrappers, & Sandwiches

Chapter Contents

CHAPTER I

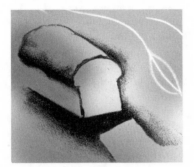

Breads
Wrappers &
Sandwiches

My first home-baked loaf of bread was a disaster, because I didn't know the difference between baking yeast and brewer's yeast. Shortly thereafter, I found the *Tassajara Bread Book,* an excellent resource. I have also found the *Cornell Bread Book* useful, with its information on protein complementing. I have included only a few of our favorite breads here. There are many books of fine recipes for bread baking; I encourage you to try some of them. I have also included a section of nonwheat breads.

One way out of the boring-lunch syndrome is to start thinking about the different forms bread can take, and even about omitting it from a sandwich altogether. One of my children's favorite lunches is what they call "toasted cheese without the bread." It is simply cheese melted on a pan and scooped up with chopsticks! I can't remember how this strange treat evolved.

You can scoop the seed cavity out of tomatoes, peppers, and cucumbers and fill. Apples and bananas (kept fresh by first dipping them in lemon juice) or cucumbers can be cut in slices with fillings sandwiched between. Raw zucchini, winter squash, or turnips can be used also. Cabbage leaves lightly steamed and nori seaweed can be used to wrap up fillings. There are many grain and nongrain foods that can be used in place of bread for sandwiches. Experiment!

Sandwich Wrapper Suggestions

muffins
rolls
bagels
matzohs
wontons
tortillas
crepes
pancakes
bread sticks
crackers
rice cakes
oat cakes

waffles
sweet breads
steamed breads
pita breads
rice paper wrappers
sliced vegetables
vegetable leaves
grape leaves
banana leaves
fruits
seaweed

Gaspé Bread

A bread my Grandpa and Grandma Bell made often. Sentimentally included. I guess they got the recipe on a trip to Nova Scotia.

>3 tablespoons honey
>2 packages active dried yeast (packages contain 1 tablespoon each)
>1 $^1/_2$ cups warm (105° to 115°F) water
>1 tablespoon butter, melted
>1 tablespoon salt
>1 cup leftover mashed potatoes
>6 cups unbleached white bread flour or white whole-wheat flour

1. In a bowl, mix honey, the 2 tablespoons yeast, and water. Let sit until foamy, 5 to 10 minutes.

2. Add butter, salt, mashed potatoes, and 1 cup of flour. Stir until smooth. Stir in the remaining flour, $^1/_2$ cup at a time until very smooth.

3. On a lightly floured board, knead for 15 minutes. Turn into an oiled bowl. Cover and let rise in a warm place for 30 minutes, or until doubled.

4. Divide in two, knead for a minute or two longer, shape into balls, and place in round baking pans. Let rise 20 minutes longer.

5. Bake in a preheated oven at 350°F for 45 minutes, or until golden.

Makes 2 round loaves

Dilled Cottage Cheese Bread

2 packages active dry yeast (packages contain 1 tablespoon each)
$1/4$ cup honey
1 $1/2$ cups warm (105° to 115°F) water
1 tablespoon butter
2 cups cottage cheese
2 teaspoons salt
$1/4$ cup dill seed
About 5 cups flour (3 cups unbleached white, 2 cups whole-wheat)

1. Mix together yeast, honey, and warm water and set aside until foamy, 5 to 10 minutes.

2. Melt butter, cool, and stir in cottage cheese. Let cool and add to yeast mixture.

3. Add salt and dill. Stir in flour $1/2$ cup at a time until a soft dough forms. Knead on a lightly floured board for 15 minutes, adding flour as needed.

4. Place in an oiled bowl. Cover and let rise in a warm place for thirty minutes, or until doubled. Punch down. Let rise for 20 minutes.

5. Divide dough in half. Shape loaves and bake in round cake pans in a preheated 350°F oven for 45 minutes, or until done. Turn the bread over and thump the bottom. If it sounds dull, there is still uncooked dough in the center. If slightly hollow sounding, the bread is baked through.

Makes 2 loaves

Bread Sticks

If you happen to be baking bread, you can easily make up a bunch of these (or let the kids do it; although they tend to get over-creative, they'll eat what they make).

Make bread dough using a standard bread recipe. Roll dough into long ropes $1/2$-inch in diameter. Cut into desired lengths and roll them in sesame or poppy seeds. Place dough on an oiled baking sheet. Cover loosely with a damp cloth and let rise in a warm place for 15 to 20 minutes, or until doubled. Bake in a preheated 350°F oven until golden brown.

Makes about 20 foot-long sticks

Zwieback

A child can chew on these on long car trips to alleviate car sickness (they will also help Mom with morning sickness), as there aren't any fats or oils as in most crackers.

Slice bread (or use presliced) about $1/2$-inch thick. Bake in a 200°F oven for 1 hour, or until toasted through. Let cool and store in airtight container.

Baking Powder Skillet Bread

We like to make this bread on camping trips to eat with hot Gluten (page 146) or Hearty Stew (page 75). In lunches, spread with spiced apple butter or cut open like biscuits and pour hot savory vegetables or Tofu in Gravy (page 80) over them.

2 cups flour ($^1/_2$ whole-wheat, $^1/_2$ unbleached white)
2 pinches salt
2 pinches baking soda
2 teaspoons baking powder
$^1/_2$ cup plain yogurt
$^1/_4$ cup water

1. Mix dry ingredients and wet ingredients separately, then mix both together.

2. Divide dough into 4 pieces. On a floured board, pat each into a flat circle $^1/_2$-inch thick.

3. Cut circles in quarters to make 16 triangles.

4. Cook in an oiled skillet over medium heat for 10 minutes on each side, or until they are golden brown.

Makes 16 wedges

Boston Brown Bread

When cool, this bread can be sliced thinly to make great sandwiches. Try with baked beans and cream cheese or baked beans and spicy mayonnaise. It can be toasted for breakfast too, and freezes well.

I cup cornmeal

I cup rye flour

I cup whole-wheat flour

I teaspoon baking soda

I teaspoon baking powder

I teaspoon salt

$1/4$ cup canola oil or melted butter (optional)

$1/2$ cup blackstrap molasses, or $3/4$ cup regular molasses

I $1/2$ cups milk or soy milk

$1/2$ cup plain yogurt

$1/2$ cup pitted dates or raisins (optional)

1. In a bowl, stir all ingredients together. Fill 2- to 3-inch diameter cans or straight-sided quart glass canning jars greased with butter two-thirds full. Cover with aluminum foil held on with a rubber band.

2. Place cans or jars on a trivet waist-deep in a pot of water and bring to a boil. Reduce heat to a simmer, cover, and cook for 1 hour (3 hours if you use 2-pound cans, or 30 minutes on a trivet in a pressure cooker).

3. Let cool. Slide a knife around insides of cans or jars to slip out bread and slice.

Makes three 2- to 3-inch diameter, 6-inch-tall loaves

Steamed Sweet Bread

This bread makes a nice cream cheese and/or peanut butter sandwich. Kids really like these rounds broiled with a little butter for breakfast. I like it with a little fruit spread.

Dry Ingredients
$1/2$ cup soy flour
1 $1/2$ cups whole-wheat flour
1 cup cornmeal
1 teaspoon salt
1 $1/2$ teaspoons baking powder
$1/2$ teaspoon ground cinnamon

Wet Ingredients
$3/4$ cup molasses or honey
1 cup water
$1/2$ cup plain yogurt

Chopped Ingredients
$1/2$ cup grated carrots
$1/2$ cup chopped dates
$1/4$ cup chopped walnuts

1. Combine dry ingredients and wet ingredients separately.

2. Mix dry and wet ingredients and fold in chopped ingredients.

3. Oil three 2- to 3-inch diameter cans, or straight-sided quart glass canning jars. Fill two-thirds to three-fourths full of batter and cover with aluminum foil held on with a rubber bank. Place on a trivet waist-deep in a pot of water.

4. Bring to a boil, reduce heat, cover, and steam for 1 hour.

5. Remove and let cool. Slide a knife around insides of cans or jars to slip out bread. Slice in rounds.

Makes 3 loaves

Branny Bran Muffins

2 $1/2$ cups bran
1 $1/2$ cups whole-wheat flour
2 tablespoons canola oil
$1/4$ cup molasses
1 cup shredded carrots
1 cup dried currants or raisins
1 $1/2$ cups apple juice
1 teaspoon ground cinnamon
$1/2$ teaspoon ground ginger
$1/2$ teaspoon ground cloves

1. In a bowl, mix all ingredients together.

2. Fill greased muffin cups two-thirds full. Bake in a preheated 350°F oven for 30 minutes, or until muffins pull away from edges or a toothpick pushed in the center comes out dry.

Makes 12 muffins

Yeasty Crepes

These evolved when a friend had phlebitis and needed to get a lot of B vitamins. I loved them when I was pregnant, for the same reason.

> I cup nutritional yeast
> I cup whole-wheat pastry flour
> About I cup water
> Spicy Mexican Vegetables (page 82) or Spicy Indian Vegetables (page 80)

1. Combine yeast and flour and add enough water to make thin batter.

2. Pour a small crepe-size amount onto a hot oiled skillet.

3. Cook until set, turn, and quickly cook other side.

4. Fill crepes with spicy vegetables and roll up. Serve at once.

Variation: Add a pinch each of ground cinnamon, ground cloves, and ground nutmeg to the batter and fill with ricotta cheese, raisins, and pecans for sweet crepes.

Makes 8 crepes; serves 4

Sesame Pancakes

Pack a dip or spread to go on these. This recipe is a good source of calcium. It contains no wheat or dairy products, and is a complementary protein to a soy spread.

> 1 cup rolled rye or rolled oats
> 4 cups water
> 1 cup millet flour (See Note)
> 1 cup sesame seed meal (See Note)
> $1/2$ teaspoon salt
> Canola oil for frying

1. Process rye or oats and water in a blender or food processor until smooth.

2. Stir in millet flour, sesame seed meal, and salt.

3. Fry in an oiled skillet over medium-low heat. Flip when golden brown.

Note: To make millet flour and sesame seed meal, grind millet, then sesame seeds, to a fine flour in a blender.

Makes 8 pancakes; serves 4

Totally Sprouted Wheat Bread

This is a very easily digested bread. Often tolerated by those who cannot tolerate wheat. It is full of vital properties.

     5 cups wheat berries
     1 cup raisins or dried apricots
     1 teaspoon salt

1. Soak wheat berries in water overnight.

2. Drain and rinse 2 times a day for 2 to 3 days, or until berries sprout and sprouts are $1/8$-inch long.

3. Grind well in a blender or food processor. Mix in dried fruit and salt. Knead on a floured board for a few minutes and let rest for 1 to 2 hours.

4. Divide dough into 10 pieces. Roll each out on a floured board to a $1/4$-inch thickness and place on an oiled pan.

5. Bake in a preheated 325°F oven for 20 minutes, or until it tests done with a tooth-pick.

Makes 10 small rolls

Totally Sprouted Wheat Chips

Prepare sprouted wheat, as above. When grinding, add enough water so that consistency is that of pancake batter. Add raisins and salt. Pour $1/4$-inch thick onto a nonstick jelly roll pan. Bake in a 200°F oven with the door cracked open for about 8 to 10 hours, or until dry. Break into chips.

Serves 6

Rice & Lentil Iddlis

These Indian breads are little pillows that can be dipped into sweet or spicy sauces. They are delicious and a good source of protein. They are most easily made using an *iddli* mold, a stand with several tiers each with 4 hollows to hold *iddli* batter. To make them without the *iddli* mold, I have used little tinfoil baking cups or individual tart molds suspended on a vegetable steaming rack inside a pot. *Iddlis* are usually eaten warm, but I like to make a large batch, freeze some, and eat the rest in my lunches all week long. I like them at room temperature.

> 2 cups long-grain white rice
> 1 cup brown lentils
> 2 cups water
> 2 teaspoons salt
> $1/_4$ teaspoon baking soda
> 1 teaspoon toasted sesame or cumin seeds (optional)

1. In separate bowls, soak rice and lentils in water to cover overnight.

2. Drain rice and grind in a blender or processor. Add 1 cup water and blend until smooth. Set aside. Grind lentils with remaining 1 cup water until smooth.

3. In a large bowl, combine rice and lentil mixtures, salt, baking soda, and optional seeds. Cover and set in a warm place for 1 day, or until batter is bubbly.

4. Oil molds and line bottom of each with parchment paper. Spoon batter into molds $1/_2$-inch thick. Put molds in a pot with 1 inch boiling water under them. Cover and steam over high heat for about 15 minutes.

Makes about 24 pillows

Pratie Oaten (Irish Potato-Oat Cakes)

My kids like these cakes with hot Welsh Rarebit (page 120) poured over them.

2 $^1/_2$ cups mashed potatoes
1 teaspoon salt
Pinch of pepper
3 cups rolled oats, ground to a course flour in a blender or food processor
Milk, as needed
Butter for cooking

1. Combine potatoes, salt, pepper, and oats, adding enough milk to make a thick dough.

2. Roll out $^1/_4$-inch thick on a floured board and cut into rounds. Melt a little butter in a hot skillet. Bake the cakes about 10 minutes per side or until lightly toasted. Oatcakes will then be dry, not soggy.

Makes about 16 oatcakes

Garbanzo Chips

Some people like these with Tofu Tartar Sauce (page 172), others with spicy sauces.

4 cups water
1 teaspoon salt
2 cups garbanzo flour (uncooked dried chickpeas ground in a blender)

1. Whisk all ingredients together in a pot. Stir over medium heat until mixture thickens and pulls away from the sides of the pot.

2. Stuff into juice cans or wide-mouth quart glass jars. Let cool and slice $^1/_4$-inch thick. Bake at 350°F for 20 minutes.

Variation: Replace garbanzo flour with cornmeal.

Makes about 24 chips

Tortillas

Place tortillas flat in a baking pan, or fold tortillas into muffin tins or taco holders and bake in a preheated 350°F oven for about 5 minutes. Top or fill with chopped raw vegetables, refried beans, grated cheese, and sour cream (pack in containers to be spooned out at lunch).

Potato Skin Nests

Cut baked potatoes in half and scoop out center. Fill skins. Poke into muffin cups and bake in a preheated 350°F oven for about 10 minutes.

All-Barley Scone

I found this chewy, flavorful scone when searching for breads made without wheat.

 1 cup yogurt
 $^1/_2$ cup water
 1 cup pearl barley
 1 $^1/_2$ cups barley
 $^1/_2$ teaspoon salt
 $^1/_2$ teaspoon baking soda

1. In a bowl, whisk the yogurt and water together. Add the pearl barley and let soak for 8 hours, or overnight.

2. In a blender or food processor, grind the other barley to make a flour. Put the barley flour, salt, and baking soda in a bowl and stir to mix. Stir in the yogurt mixture until blended. Spoon the mixture into an oiled small cast-iron skillet. Bake in a preheated 350°F oven for about 45 minutes, or until golden brown.

Oatcakes

Try these with jam or apple butter and thin slices of Cheddar cheese.

1 $1/2$ cups rolled oats, ground in a blender or food processor
$1/8$ teaspoon baking soda
2 pinches salt
1 tablespoon butter, melted (optional)
About $1/3$ cup hot water

1. In a bowl, mix dry ingredients together. Pour optional melted butter over. Gradually stir in enough hot water to form a thick dough. Form into 8 to 12 balls.

2. On a lightly floured board, roll out each ball into a round $1/8$-inch thick.

3. Cut each round into quarters. Place on a baking sheet and bake in a preheated 350°F oven for 20 minutes, or until golden brown, crisp, and light. Or, cook on an ungreased skillet for 10 minutes each side.

Makes 8 to 12 oatcakes; serves 4

Pizza Turnovers

For the crust, use your favorite bread dough.

On a lightly floured board, roll out bread dough to a little more than $1/8$-inch thick. Cut into 5-inch squares. Fill with grated cheese, tomato sauce, and whatever vegetables you like. Fold over and seal edges. Bake in a preheated 350°F oven until golden, about 15 to 20 minutes.

Variations: Other vegetable turnovers might include Chili con Veg (page 78), potpie filling (page 118), Gluten (page 146), or Spicy Mexican Vegetables (page 82).

Vegetable Braid

This is good to pack for a family picnic.

When baking bread, after the first rising, set aside a softball-sized lump of dough for a vegetable braid. On a lightly floured board, roll bread dough out to 1/2-inch-thick rectangle. Make slits along the sides. Fill with a thick, flavorful filling. Fold sides in, overlapping each other. Bake in a preheated 350°F oven for 45 minutes, or until golden brown.

Makes 1 braid; serves 4 to 6

Strollers

Slice a piece of pita bread in half horizontally to make 2 thin flat rounds. Place some filling and shredded vegetables on each and roll up. Roll each bread in waxed paper, tucking ends in as you roll. To eat, just peel down from top as you go.

Makes 1 stroller; serves 1

Bread Nests

Nests are crisp little hollow forms that hold fillings.

Cut crusts from a slice of bread (save crust for making burgers). With a rolling pin, roll out bread slightly. Butter both sides lightly and push into muffin tin. Repeat for more nests. Bake in a preheated 350°F oven for about 20 minutes, or until golden and crisp. Send filling in a thermos and fill the nest at eating time (the nests will get soggy if pre-filled; they store well for 2 days).

Makes 1 nest; serves 1

Sandwich Log

My youngest child is very fond of these. She says that they are valuable trade items. These can be eaten as a log or cut into 1-inch-thick slices to make pinwheels.

Cut crusts off a slice of bread. Roll out with a rolling pin and spread with any filling the consistency of softened cream cheese. Roll up into a log.

Make 1 log; serves 1

Filo Sandwiches

Buy frozen packaged filo or make your own.

Cut 2 sheets filo leaves into 4-inch-wide strips. Place filling in one corner and fold in triangle fashion (like folding a flag) the length of the strip. Brush outside with melted butter, sprinkle with sesame or poppy seeds, and bake in a preheated 350°F oven until golden.

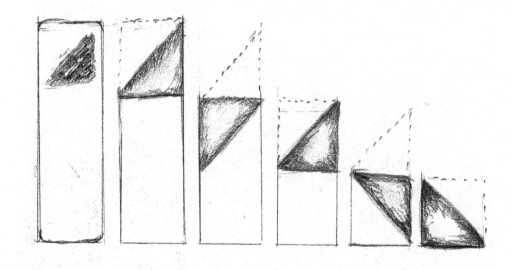

Makes 2 sandwiches; serves 1

Rice Paper Packets

These are fun to make on a picnic. They are light enough that you will have no problem jumping up for a volleyball game. They are also a very intriguing food. The filling is my favorite dish. I could eat it (and have) for breakfast, lunch, and dinner for days on end.

Filling

1 package dried flat tofu skin

1 head savoy cabbage, cored and shredded

3 cups cooked chopped spinach

1 green bell pepper, seeded, deribbed, and chopped

6 squares aromatic dried bean curd

$1/4$ cup tomato puree

3 tablespoons Asian sesame oil

1 teaspoon chili oil

3 tablespoons grated fresh ginger

2 teaspoons salt

1 tablespoon tamari sauce

24 square rice paper wrappers

Chopped fresh cilantro (optional)

1. Before opening package, break up tofu skin into 2-inch or smaller flakes. Add to a saucepan of boiling water and cook for 10 minutes. Drain.

2. Cook vegetables in a small amount of water until almost tender. Drain.

3. Toss together vegetables, bean curd, tofu skin, tomato puree, oils, ginger, salt, and tamari.

4. To serve, set out a bowl of rice papers and a little bowl of cilantro. Dip each rice paper in a bowl of water and stack on a plate. They will continue to soften. Everyone takes a wrapper, fills it, folds in 3 sides, and rolls it up like a cigar. These can be eaten plain or dipped into a sauce such as tamari and ginger, or peanut sauce.

Makes 24 pockets; serves 6

Bean & Cheese Tamales

These are fun to bring on a camping trip. They can be grilled and munched with a salsa. They are also fine heated in an office microwave.

Crust
3 cups masa harina
3 tablespoons canola oil
2 teaspoons salt
2 cups water
1 teaspoon chili powder
10 dried corn husks, (soaked in water for 30 minutes and drained)

Filling
2 cups corn kernels
1 cup cooked pinto beans
1 cup shredded smoked mozzarella or Cheddar cheese
$1/_2$ teaspoon salt
1 teaspoon chili powder
2 tablespoons chopped fresh cilantro
$1/_2$ cup roasted sweet or hot peppers

1. In a bowl, mix all crust ingredients together and knead for about 10 minutes.

2. On each husk, spread some crust mixture about $1/_3$-inch thick.

3. Combine all filling ingredients. In center of each husk, spread a few tablespoons of filling. Fold sides of husks over to make a fat cigar shape. Fold ends over next, and tie closed or place fold side down on steamer.

4. Steam tamales over boiling water in a covered pot for 1 hour.

Makes 10 tamales; serves 5

Dolmas (Stuffed Grape Leaves)

I first tasted these when Haley, a student of mine, brought them to our fifth grade Greek feast. I must have eaten almost half of them. A few weeks later, I finally noticed all the wild grapevines that run rampant around here. I picked several leaves and made supper. They were so good that I picked hundreds to blanch and freeze for winter.

15 grape leaves, preferably young 4- to 5-inches across
1 teaspoon salt
1 cup mashed cooked adzuki beans
$1/2$ cup half-cooked rice
2 tablespoons olive oil
2 tablespoons pine nuts, sesame seeds, walnuts, or almonds
Juice of 2 lemons

1. Blanch grape leaves in salted boiling water for 3 minutes. Set aside.

2. Mix beans, rice, oil, and nuts together. Put a dollop of filling on under side of a leaf and fold leaf over. Fold ends in and roll up like a cigar.

3. Layer dolmas in a heavy pot. Add water to an inch from top. Put a plate on top to hold down the dolmas.

4. Simmer for 30 minutes. Remove and let cool. Drizzle lemon juice over all.

Makes 15 dolmas; serves 4

Filled Lotus, Bamboo, or Grape Leaves

These are interesting to make. A few years ago, I planted some North American lotuses in pots in our pond. They escaped their pots, threatening our swimming space. I consider eating these good ecological control. It may be possible to purchase these or bamboo leaves in an Asian market. Grape leaves are obtainable from nature or a regular grocery store.

I small globe eggplant
I cup glutinous rice
I cup water
$1/2$ cup dried chestnuts
$1/4$ cup raw peanuts
$1/4$ cup bamboo shoots
I teaspoon molasses
$1/2$ teaspoon salt
2 teaspoons tamari sauce
Few drops chili oil to taste
2 teaspoons Asian sesame oil
I tablespoon chopped fresh chives
2 large lotus leaves, or 8 bamboo or grape leaves

1. Roast eggplant in a 350°F oven until tender, about 30 minutes. Let cool. Peel and cut into $1/2$-inch dice.

2. Rinse and drain rice. Put it in a pan with the water. Put this pan in a large pot on a trivet. Add 2 inches water to pot, bring to a boil, reduce heat to a simmer, cover, and steam rice for 30 minutes.

3. Cook dried chestnuts in boiling water until tender, about 20 minutes. Drain. Cut into fourths. Cook peanuts in boiling water until tender, about 15 minutes.

4. Mix all ingredients except leaves together and mound it on 1 lotus leaf or divide among bamboo or grape leaves. Cover with the second leaf and fold all the edges under. Place this packet on a steaming rack. Steam for about 30 minutes. Eat filling from a hole cut in middle of leaf.

Makes 2 large lotus leaf packets or 8 bamboo or grape leaf packets; serves 4

Celery Logs

My thoughtful mom made these for a long car trip I took. They are easily digested and easily held while driving.

> 1 cup Yogurt Cheese (page 51)
> 2 tablespoons dried vegetable flakes
> $1/2$ teaspoon salt
> 18 celery stalks

1. Mix all ingredients but the celery together.

2. Cut celery into long stalks. Stuff one stalk, mounding middle.

3. Press another stalk of equal length over it so that mound fills cavities.

4. Tie ends with rubber bands and refrigerate for at least 4 hours.

Makes 9 logs; serves 3

Lettuce Rolls

These rolls have a great Thai taste. They can be assembled ahead, but everyone loves free choice. Leisurely play at the table is great for family bonding.

Sauce
1 cup molasses
1 teaspoon salt
2 teaspoons tamari sauce
3 tablespoons chopped fresh chives
$1/2$ cup shredded dried coconut, toasted
4 tablespoons grated fresh ginger
1 cup water
1 tablespoon chopped fresh parsley
$1/4$ teaspoon chili oil
1 tablespoon raisins
1 tablespoon lime juice
1 head iceberg or romaine lettuce or 12 leaves of leaf lettuce
$1/4$ cup minced fresh ginger
$1/2$ cup coconut, toasted
$1/2$ cup salted dry-roasted peanuts
$1/4$ cup salted toasted pumpkin or sunflower seeds
$1/4$ cup chopped fresh chives
$1/4$ cup thinly sliced Thai (or substitute what you have) chiles

1. Combine all sauce ingredients in a blender and puree. Put in a small saucepan, bring to a simmer, and cook for about 15 minutes. Let cool.

2. Set out each of the remaining ingredients in a separate bowl or on a platter in separate piles. Everyone takes a lettuce leaf and arranges a little of each of the separate components on it. A little sauce is spooned on and the leaf is folded into a little package to be popped into their mouths.

Makes about 12 rolls; serves 4

CHAPTER 2

Fillings & Spreads

Chapter Contents

CHAPTER 2

Fillings
&
Spreads

These fillings can be sandwiched or stuffed into wrappings or packed in a container to be eaten with chips or a spoon. Some are sweet and some are spicy, but most of them are a good source of protein. Be sure to try adding snips of your favorite fresh herbs. I've made suggestions, but you should us your own favorite herbs.

Sandwich Suggestions

Pestofu (page 45) and tomato on a croissant

Apple butter and mild Cheddar cheese on oatmeal bread

Sliced avocado and Honey-Fried Tofu (page 148) on Baking Powder Skillet Bread (page 8)

Sliced avocado, Spicy Mexican Vegetables (page 82), and mayonnaise on a croissant

Sliced avocado and powdered pecans (pecans you have whizzed in a blender until they are turned to a powder) in Sandwich Logs (page 20)

Basic Burger (page 150), mayonnaise, tomato, lettuce, pickle, ketchup, and mustard on a sesame seed bun

Sunflower seeds, mayonnaise, grated cheese, and tomato on Oatcakes (page 18)

Yogurt Cheese (page 51) and chopped green olives on oatmeal bread

Yogurt Cheese and chopped pineapple on Steamed Sweet Bread (page 10)

Yogurt Cheese and Peach Chutney (page 160) on waffles

Yogurt Cheese and fresh chopped herbs in a Sandwich Log (page 20)

Yogurt Cheese and Marinated Vegetables (page 92) on rice cakes

Yogurt Cheese and pecans on pancakes

Yogurt Cheese, Mama Papa's Peppers (page 92), and black olives on tortillas

Yogurt Cheese, mashed avocado, and Lemon-Honey Jelly (page 167) on matzohs

Yogurt Cheese on Steamed Sweet Bread (page 10) or Vegetable Braid (page 19)

Feta cheese and chopped pecans in a Sandwich Log (page 20)

Asparagus spears and Tofu Mayonnaise (page 164) in a Sandwich Log (page 20)

French Toast or waffles with Lemon-Honey Jelly (page 167)

Golden Tofu Nuggets (page 121) and Lemon-Honey Jelly (page 167) on crackers

Split Pea Spread (page 39), Spicy Tofu Mayonnaise (page 164), and black olives on corn bread

Split Pea Spread (page 39), Tahini Cheese Spread (page 41), tomato, and sprouts in pita pockets

Grated cheese, mayonnaise, and chopped raw cauliflower on Garbanzo Chips (page 16)

Sliced cucumbers and Tofu Mayonnaise (page 164) on oatmeal bread

Guacamole on corn chips

Vermont Nut Loaf (page 144) and mayonnaise on Oatcakes (page 18)

Honey-Fried Tofu (page 148) and Spicy Tofu Mayonnaise (page 164) in pita Strollers (page 20)

Refried Bean Spread (page 38), tomato slices, grated jack cheese, and sour cream in a Tortilla Nest (page 20)

Brown Gluten (page 146) and sauerkraut on matzoh

Brown Gluten (page 146), lettuce, tomato, and mayonnaise on rye

Gluten (page 146) cooked in Sea Broth (page 70), with Tofu Tartar Sauce (page 172) in a pita Stroller (page 20)

Mashed Lentil Spread (page 39) with Mama Papa's Peppers (page 92), avocado, and Parmesan cheese on rice cakes

Soy Scrapple (page 132) and sauerkraut on croissant horns

Peanut butter and apple butter in a Sandwich Log (page 20)

Peanut butter and cheese slices on oatmeal bread

Peanut butter and cooked mashed parsnips on Steamed Sweet Bread (page 10)

Peanut butter and Yogurt Cheese (page 51) rolled in Yeasty Crepes (page 12)

Peanut butter and D.V.'s Mincemeat (page 162) on Boston Brown Bread (page 9)

Peanut butter, chopped celery, and mayonnaise on bagels

Peanut butter, roasted almonds, chopped celery, and mayonnaise on Steamed Sweet Bread (page 10)

Peanut butter, Tofu Mayonnaise (page 164), grated carrots, and raisins on muffins

Sliced cooked beets and Tofu Mayonnaise (page 164) on Gaspé Bread (page 5)

Baked Tofu (page 133) and tartar sauce with capers on matzoh

Baked Tofu (page 133), mayonnaise, and tomato on rye bread

Sliced tomatoes and Tofu Mayonnaise (page 164) in pita pockets

Hummus (page 35) and Mama Papa's Peppers (page 92) on rice cakes

Hummus (page 35), sprouts, and tomato on pita bread

Sunflower seeds, Tofu Mayonnaise (page 164), and mashed Artichoke Heart Delight (page 47) on a croissant

Tofu Tartar Sauce (page 172), cheese slices, and cucumbers on crackers

Yellow Gluten (page 146) and Cranberry Ketchup (page 159) in a tortilla

Baked beans and Yogurt Cheese (page 51) on Boston Brown Bread (page 9)

Baked beans, Dijon mustard, and Tofu Mayonnaise (page 164) on Boston Brown Bread (page 9)

Hummus

This is usually eaten on pita bread, but it can also be used as a sauce on Spicy Indian Vegetables (page 80).

2 cups cooked chickpeas (garbanzo beans) with $3/4$ cups of their water
$1/2$ cup tahini
2 tablespoons fresh lemon juice
1 teaspoon dried dill or ground cumin
Salt to taste

Combine all ingredients in a blender or food processor and process until smooth. Keeps for about 5 days in a covered container in the refrigerator.

Makes about 2 cups

Nutto Spread

Use sparingly, as this is high in fat.

$1/2$ cup Tofu Mayonnaise (page 164)
$1/2$ cup cashew butter or tahini
$1/2$ cup finely chopped celery
$1/2$ cup chopped pitted olives
$1/2$ cup chopped pecans

In a bowl, stir all ingredients together. Keeps about 5 to 7 days in a covered container in the refrigerator.

Makes about 2 cups

Split Pea & Cheese Spread

1 cup Split Pea Spread (page 39)
1 cup shredded Cheddar cheese
$1/2$ cup Spicy Tofu Mayonnaise (page 164)
Snipped fresh dill, cilantro, or rosemary to taste (optional)

In a bowl, combine all ingredients. Serve at room temperature or heated. Store in a covered container in the refrigerator for about 5 days.

Makes about 1 $3/4$ cups

Cheese-Eggplant Spread

Delicious in a pita Stroller (page 20), wrapped in a flour tortilla, or stuffed in vegetables. Use sparingly — this is not low in fat.

$1/4$ cup olive oil
2 large globe eggplants, peeled and cubed
$1/4$ head cabbage, cored and chopped
1 green bell pepper, seeded, deribbed, and chopped
1 cup toasted hazelnuts, chopped
1 teaspoon salt or to taste
1 cup shredded Cheddar cheese

1. In a large skillet, heat olive oil over medium heat and sauté cabbage and green pepper for about 5 minutes.

2. Add eggplants, hazelnuts, and salt. Cover and simmer gently until soft, about 10 minutes.

3. Let cool for a minute or two. Crush slightly while mixing in cheese.

Makes about 4 cups

Peanut-Yeast Spread

This high-protein spread is good in sandwiches with tomatoes and sprouts.

$1/2$ cup peanut butter
$1/2$ cup Tofu Mayonnaise (page 164)
$1/4$ cup nutritional yeast

In a bowl, mix all ingredients together. Keeps about 1 week covered in a container in the refrigerator.

Makes about 1 cup

Tofunut Spread

3 tablespoons boiling water
3 tablespoons peanut butter
8 ounces firm tofu
Pinch of salt

1. In a blender or food processor, blend water and peanut butter.

2. Add tofu and salt. Process until smooth. Keep in a covered container in the refrigerator for up to 5 days.

Makes $3/4$ cup

Refried Bean Spread

1 cup cooked pinto beans
$^{1}/_{2}$ teaspoon ground cumin
$^{1}/_{4}$ teaspoon salt
Pinch of cayenne
Canola oil for cooking

1. Gently mash beans.

2. Stir in cumin, salt, and cayenne. Let cool.

3. In an oiled skillet over medium heat, cook until mixture begins to dry and firm up. Store in a covered container in the refrigerator for up to 5 days.

Makes 1 cup

Cheddar Spread

This is good hot or cold. Try some spread on an English muffin and broiled.

1 cup shredded Cheddar cheese
$^{1}/_{2}$ cup Tofu Mayonnaise (page 164)

In a bowl, stir ingredients together. Keeps up to 1 week in refrigerator in a covered container.

Variation: Add 1 teaspoon snipped fresh dill or 2 tablespoons chopped dill pickle.

Makes about 1 $^{1}/_{4}$ cups

Sesame-Avocado Spread

$1/_4$ cup tahini

1 teaspoon tamari sauce

3 tablespoons hot water

Juice of 1 lemon

1 avocado peeled, pitted, and diced

$1/_4$ teaspoon paprika

1. In a bowl, mix tahini, tamari, water, and lemon juice.

2. Add the avocado and paprika and mash well. Cover and keep in the refrigerator until serving. Best if eaten within 2 days.

Makes about 1 cup

Lentil, Mung Bean, or Split Pea Spread

This is a simple, mild spread that readily accepts lots of spices or herbs.

1 cup dried lentils, mung beans, or split peas

2 cups water

Salt to taste

1. Combine legumes and water in a saucepan. Bring to a boil, reduce heat to low, and simmer until soft, about 45 minutes. Drain.

2. In a blender, puree to the consistency of applesauce. Add salt. Store in a covered container in refrigerator for up to 5 days.

Variations:

Add $1/_4$ cup Yogurt Cheese (page 51) and 1 tablespoon curry powder.

Add $1/_4$ cup minced fresh cilantro leaves and a squeeze of lemon juice.

Add $^1/_4$ cup snipped fresh chives and a squeeze of lemon juice.

Add $^1/_4$ cup Yogurt Cheese (page 51) and 2 tablespoons minced fresh dill weed.

Makes 1 $^1/_2$ to 2 cups

Split Pea & Tahini Dip

1 cup Split Pea Spread (page 39)
2 tablespoons fresh lemon juice
$^1/_2$ cup tahini
1 teaspoon soy sauce
2 tablespoons grated Parmesan cheese

In a bowl, stir all ingredients together. Serve hot or cold. Store in a covered container in the refrigerator for up to 5 days.

Makes about 1 $^1/_2$ cups

Vegnut Spread

1 cup Tofu Mayonnaise (page 164)
1 cup peanut butter
$^1/_2$ cup shredded carrots
$^1/_2$ cup finely chopped celery
$^1/_2$ cup finely chopped green bell pepper

1. In a bowl, mix mayonnaise and peanut butter.

2. Stir in vegetables. Keep in a covered container in the refrigerator for up to 5 days.

Makes about 2 $^1/_2$ cups

Tahini-Cheese Spread

This can also be mixed with hot vegetables or used in place of mayonnaise in a vegetable or burger sandwich.

$3/4$ cups Yogurt Cheese (page 51)
2 to 3 tablespoons tahini
Dash of tamari sauce
Hot water as needed

In a bowl, mash all ingredients together. Store in a covered container in the refrigerator for up to 5 days. Best if eaten within 3 days.

Makes $3/4$ cup

Chickpea Salad

3 cups cooked chickpeas (garbanzo beans)
1 cup Yogurt Cheese (page 51)
1 cup cottage cheese
2 cups chopped celery
Salt and pepper to taste

1. Mash chickpeas and yogurt cheese together until all chickpeas are at least broken in half.

2. Stir in all remaining ingredients.

3. Refrigerate for at least 2 hours. Thin with milk if needed.

Variation: Add 1 tablespoon curry powder before refrigerating.

Makes about 5 cups

Baba Ghanoush

This is delicious stuffed in fresh tomatoes, eaten on pita bread with sliced tomatoes, or dipped on rye crackers.

> 1 globe eggplant
> 1 teaspoon salt
> 2 tablespoons chopped fresh chives (optional)
> 5 tablespoons fresh lemon juice
> 3 tablespoons chopped fresh parsley
> Pinch of pepper
> 3 tablespoons olive oil
> $1/_4$ cup Yogurt Cheese (page 51) or 1 tablespoon tahini

1. Bake eggplant in a preheated 375°F oven until skin blisters, about 20 minutes. Let cool. Peel and chop eggplant.

2. Mix eggplant with all remaining ingredients.

3. Let sit overnight to meld the flavors. Keeps 5 days in a covered container in refrigerator.

Makes about 1 $3/_4$ cups

Tofu Pâté

This is nice stuffed in croissants or spread on crackers.

  I pound firm tofu
  I cup green beans, trimmed and chopped
  3 tablespoons Tofu Mayonnaise (page 164)
  $^1/_2$ cup walnuts, ground to flour in a blender or food processor
  I tablespoon dry white wine
  1/2 teaspoon Dijon-style mustard
  2 pinches hing (asafetida)
  $^3/_4$ teaspoon salt

Process all ingredients together in blender or food processor. Refrigerate for at least 2 hours. Store in a covered container in the refrigerator for up to 5 days.

Makes about 2 $^1/_2$ cups

Chestnut Salata

Chestnuts are low in fat and high in flavor. Try this spread on rice cakes or baked crackers or chips.

  I pound chestnuts
  I cup plain yogurt
  I tablespoon chopped fresh chives
  I tablespoon chopped fresh cilantro
  I teaspoon salt

I. Take chestnuts and make an X on the shell. Simmer in water to cover about 30 minutes. Peel while warm and mash in a blender or food processor. In a bowl, mix all ingredients together. Keep in a covered container in the refrigerator for up to I week.

Makes about 2 $^1/_2$ cups

Tofu Salad

This very simple spread is delicious, dairy-free, and reminiscent of egg salad. This is my favorite sandwich filling.

>   1 pound firm drained tofu, mashed
>   1 cup Tofu Mayonnaise (page 164)
>   1 cup chopped celery
>   Salt and pepper to taste

In a bowl, mix all ingredients together. Keeps in a covered container in the refrigerator for 5 days to 1 week.

Makes about 2 cups

Fruit Spread

>   4 cups chopped mixed dried fruits (prunes, raisins, apricots, dates, peaches, apples, or pineapples)
> $1/2$ cup grated carrots
>   1 teaspoon salt
> $1/3$ cup fresh lemon juice
>   1 teaspoon grated lemon zest
>   1 $1/2$ cups water

1. In a saucepan, combine all ingredients and simmer gently for 1 hour.

2. Puree in a blender.

3. Simmer again until thick, about 45 minutes. Keeps 1 week in a covered container in the refrigerator.

Makes about 5 cups

Corn & Tomato Salsa

Try this with polenta or garbanzo chips.

> 1 tablespoon olive oil
> $1/4$ teaspoon chili oil (optional)
> 5 teaspoons cider vinegar
> 1 teaspoon ground cumin
> 1 tablespoon chopped fresh chives
> $1/2$ cup chopped fresh cilantro
> 1 cup cooked corn kernels
> 3 cups chopped tomatoes
> 1 cup roasted mild green chilies

1. In a bowl, mix oils, vinegar, cumin, chives, and cilantro.

2. Pour onto vegetables and stir together. Store in a covered container in the refrigerator. Best if eaten within a day or two.

Makes about 5 cups

Pestofu

Our community farm always has an abundance of basil, so I make lots of pesto. Since it is so flavorful, my youngest child thought I ought to thin it out with our universal mixer: tofu. It works wonderfully. We like it on pasta or as a dip for breads and baked crackers and chips.

> 1 pound firm tofu, drained and chopped
> 1 $1/2$ cups Pesto Sentio (page 168)
> $1/2$ cup tomato puree
> 2 teaspoons tamari sauce

Puree all ingredients in a blender until smooth. Store in a covered container in the refrigerator for up to 3 to 4 days.

Makes about 3 cups

Sesame-Yogurt Sauce

This is a flavorful, but mild sauce. It goes well with spicy foods.

$^1/_4$ cup fresh lemon juice
$^1/_2$ cup plain yogurt
$^1/_4$ cup tahini
2 pinches salt

In a bowl, stir all ingredients together. Store in a covered container in the refrigerator for up to 5 days.

Makes about 1 cup

Yeast Spread

This is high in protein and B vitamins.

$^1/_2$ cup Tofu Mayonnaise (page 164)
$^1/_4$ cup nutritional yeast
$^1/_4$ teaspoon prepared mustard (Dijon style tastes nice, but mild yellow is fine)
3 tablespoons minced sweet pickles or relish
1 tablespoon capers or pickled nasturtium buds

In a bowl, stir all ingredients together. Keeps in a covered container in the refrigerator for up to 3 days.

Makes about $^3/_4$ cup

Creamed Honey

When honey comes into contact with air, it crystallizes into a grainy texture. When whipped, the honey grows tiny crystals, resulting in a creamy texture.

This makes a nice, thick spread that can be spiced if desired and used with nut butters for a sandwich spread. (Save out 1 cup for making the next batch.)

> 1 cup creamed honey
> 6 cups regular honey

1. In a blender or with a mixer, blend the two honeys until combined and whipped.

2. Place in a covered container for a few weeks until very tiny crystals begin to grow. The crystals are so small that the honey will be creamy rather than grainy. Keeps indefinitely.

Makes 7 cups

Artichoke Hearts Delight

These are delicious stuffed into croissants.

> 6 artichoke hearts (I use canned, but frozen would also work, if available)
> $1/3$ cup Yogurt Cheese (page 51)
> $1/2$ cup Tofu Mayonnaise (page 164)
> 2 tablespoons grated Parmesan cheese

1. Heat artichoke hearts in a saucepan. Remove from heat and mash slightly.

2. Add the remaining ingredients and blend. Keeps in a covered container in the refrigerator for about 1 week.

Makes about 1 $1/2$ cups

Molasses-Tahini Spread

A friend sent us a case of carob syrup from Cypress, and not knowing what to do with it, we tried it in place of the molasses. If you have carob syrup, it is a nice alternative. This is great on pumpernickel.

    1 cup molasses
    3 tablespoons tahini

In a bowl, blend ingredients together. Store in a covered container in the refrigerator for up to 2 weeks.

Makes 1 $^1/_4$ cups

Chickpea Soufflé Spread

    1 cup Chickpea Soufflé (page 125)
    $^1/_2$ cup pine nuts
    $^1/_4$ cup mayonnaise or Tofu Mayonnaise (page 164)
    $^1/_4$ cup chopped celery
    $^1/_4$ cup sweet pickle relish

In a bowl, mix all ingredients together. Store in a covered container in the refrigerator for up to a week.

Makes about 2 cups

Thai Peanut Sauce

A high-protein sauce that is great at a cookout. Dip vegetable kabobs in it or spread it on rice cakes or chips.

1 cup coconut milk
$1/_2$ cup water
1 tablespoon dried vegetable flakes
$1/_2$ teaspoon salt
3 tablespoons molasses
1 tablespoon grated fresh ginger
1 teaspoon hing (asafetida)
1 teaspoon cumin seed, ground
6 small hot roasted jalapeño chilies
$1/_4$ cup peanut butter
2 tablespoons fresh lime juice

1. Combine all ingredients except peanut butter and lime juice in a small saucepan. Bring to a boil, reduce heat to low, and simmer for about 10 minutes.

2. Add peanut butter and simmer for a few minutes.

3. Puree in a blender. Stir in lime juice. Store in a covered container in the refrigerator for up to 1 week.

Makes about 2 cups

Olive-Tomato Pesto

Great on pasta or polenta chips.

$^1/_2$ teaspoon hing (asafetida)
$^1/_2$ cup tomato paste
2 tablespoons olive oil
$^1/_2$ teaspoon dried marjoram
2 cups black olives, pitted

1. Combine hing and tomato paste in a small saucepan. Bring to a boil, reduce heat, and simmer for 3 minutes. Let cool.

2. Combine tomato mixture and all remaining ingredients in a blender or food processor and puree. Keeps in a covered container in the refrigerator for about a week.

Makes about 1 cup

Thai Eggplant Sauce

Raw vegetables taste wonderful dipped into this zesty sauce. It also is good on *iddlis* or garbanzo chips.

1 large globe eggplant
2 tablespoons fresh lime juice
2 teaspoons tamari sauce
2 tablespoons molasses
2 tablespoons minced jalapeño chilies
2 tablespoons chopped fresh chives
4 tablespoons chopped fresh cilantro

1. Roast eggplant in a preheated 375°F oven for 20 minutes, or until browned and tender.

2. Peel and mash. Combine eggplant, lime juice, tamari, molasses, and chilies in a blender and puree until smooth.

3. Stir in chives and cilantro. Store in a covered container in the refrigerator. Best if eaten the next day, but keeps 3 to 5 days.

Makes about 2 cups

Yogurt Cheese

Use this in place of mayonnaise or cream cheese. It is high in protein and is wonderful for the digestion.

Drain plain low-fat yogurt in a sieve lined with 2 layers of cheesecloth for 3 to 8 hours.

Variations: Mix Yogurt Cheese with dried vegetable flakes and a pinch of salt. Let sit overnight. Or, add minced fresh herbs and a pinch of salt.

Sesame Salt (Goma-shio)

According to my daughter, Haven, everything tastes better with a little *goma-shio* sprinkled on it.

    1 $^1/_2$ cups sesame seeds, toasted and ground to cornmeal consistency
    3 teaspoons salt

In a bowl, mix sesame seeds and salt well. Store in a jar. This keeps for several weeks, but I prefer to keep the toasted sesame seeds whole and grind only a week's worth of them at one time.

Makes about 1 $^1/_2$ cups

CHAPTER 3

Soups & Thermos Foods

Chapter Contents

CHAPTER 3

Soups & Thermos Foods

On cold winter days, it's nice to have a hot lunch. A hot sauce over an open-faced sandwich is one good warmup for a cold day. Bring the sauce in a thermos and pour it over a sandwich, chips, or burgers when lunchtime arrives. This will keep the sauce hot and the food from getting soggy.

There are many vegetables that my daughters would not eat when they were younger (and my son still won't), but shredded into soups they now like them just fine. As Jamie, at age four, explained to my mother when she was attempting to feed him vegetables, "Just shred them small enough so that I can't find them or cut them big enough so that I can fling them out."

Plastic thermoses don't work as well as the glass-lined ones. The food cools down too quickly, and if not, sometimes the top swells and sticks. Still, these don't break. I have a friend who wraps hot food in towels and puts it in a cooler. (Much like the old" hot boxes" of the 1800s.) Her food always arrives at potlucks hot and melty, even if there's been a long social or meditative hour before dinner. If you use this "hot box" method of transport, be aware that food continues to slow cook. If this involves pasta, potatoes, or other foods that can cook to mush, prepare them a little on the undercooked side.

Cabbage Soup

1 cabbage, cored and shredded

2 cups water

2 cups milk

2 tablespoons flour

1 cup mashed potatoes

3 tablespoons butter

Salt and pepper to taste

1 cup grated Parmesan cheese

1. In a saucepan, bring water to a boil. Add cabbage, reduce heat, and simmer until almost soft, about 15 minutes.

2. Combine milk, flour, and potatoes in a bowl. Add to cabbage. Simmer for 5 to 10 minutes.

3. Season to taste (under-salt because of the later addition of Parmesan cheese).

4. Add Parmesan to thermos when packing.

Serves 4

Tofu-Noodle Soup

This is our vegetarian version of chicken noodle soup.

> 3 cups water
> 2 tablespoons chopped celery
> 1 tablespoon chopped fresh parsley
> 4 ounces linguine, broken into 2-inch lengths
> 1 pound extra-firm or firm tofu, chopped fine
> 1 tablespoon nutritional yeast
> 2 teaspoons butter

In a soup pot, bring water to a boil. Add all remaining ingredients and simmer for 25 to 35 minutes, or until noodles are tender.

Serves 4

Lentil Soup

Leftover lentil soup can be used in Basic Burgers (page 150) or Pepper Pot Soup (page 60), or it can be frozen.

> 2 tablespoons olive oil
> 1 cup chopped cabbage
> 1 cup chopped green bell pepper
> 2 cups dried lentils
> 5 cups water or more
> 2 teaspoons cumin seed
> 1 carrot, peeled and grated
> 2 tablespoons tamari sauce
> Pinch of pepper
> Salt to taste
> Grated Parmesan cheese for garnish

1. In a soup pot, heat oil over medium heat and sauté cabbage and green pepper until tender, about 5 minutes.

2. Add all remaining ingredients except Parmesan cheese. Bring to a boil, reduce heat to low, and simmer for 40 minutes. Serve garnished with Parmesan.

Serves 5

Minestrone

This is a wonderfully versatile soup. Use any vegetables, beans, pasta, or grains. After an Italian supper, chop up all the pasta (with sauce on it) and the antipasto and simmer all together.

> 2 cups water
> $1/2$ cup each chopped carrots, peas, and chopped potatoes
> 2 stalks celery, chopped
> $1/2$ cup chopped cabbage
> 1 cup chopped spinach
> 4 ounces pasta
> $1/2$ cup cooked chickpeas
> $1/2$ cup cooked kidney beans
> 2 tablespoons olive oil
> 1 cup tomato puree
> $1/4$ cup grated Parmesan cheese
> $1/2$ teaspoon dried marjoram
> $1/2$ teaspoon dried thyme

1. In a soup pot, bring water to a boil and add vegetables and pasta. Reduce heat to low, cover, and simmer for 35 minutes.

2. Add all remaining ingredients and simmer for 10 minutes.

Serves 6

Squash-Cheese Soup

1 teaspoons butter
3 tablespoons whole-wheat flour
2 cups milk or vegetable stock
1 cup shredded sharp Cheddar cheese
2 cups cooked winter squash, mashed
Salt and pepper to taste

1. In a saucepan, melt butter over medium-low heat and whisk in flour. Stir for 3 minutes. Gradually stir in milk or stock. Simmer until thickened.

2. Stir in cheese, squash, salt, and pepper. Simmer for 5 minutes.

Serves 4

Note: I have included cheese in several recipes. It is not really low in fat, so I usually eat it about once a week. I find that a topping or garnish of cheese will still deliver flavor without indulging in too much fat.

For a delicious lowfat, high-protein soup, try this simple version:

1 pound firm tofu
2 cups cooked winter squash (in summer I use cold pre-cooked summer squash or zucchini for a cold soup)

In a blender, puree until smooth. Add salt and pepper to taste. Garnish with snips of parsley or cilantro and toasted sesame seeds.

Corn Chowder

2 large potatoes (red or white), scrubbed and chopped

3 cups corn kernels

$^1/_2$ cup chopped celery (include some leaves)

2 tablespoons texturized vegetable protein (TVP), or 1 cup chopped
   frozen tofu (optional)

1 cup water

1 cup milk or soy milk or nut milk

Salt and pepper to taste

1 tablespoon butter

1. In a large saucepan, combine vegetables, TVP or tofu and water. Bring to a boil, reduce heat to low, cover, and simmer until tender, about 25 minutes.

2. Add milk, salt, pepper, and butter. Simmer for 10 minutes.

Note: Frozen tofu has a chewy texture, because the water in it has frozen in tiny grains leaving a high protein sponge-like soy substance.

Serves 3

Pepper Pot Soup

2 cups water

3 carrots, peeled and sliced

1 turnip, cubed

1 tomato, chopped

1 zucchini, chopped

1 tablespoon chopped fresh parsley

1 cup cooked lentils, pureed

$^1/_4$ cup tamari sauce, or 1 tablespoon miso

Salt to taste

Lots of freshly ground black pepper

1. In a soup pot, bring water to a boil. Add vegetables and simmer until tender, about 25 minutes.

2. Add lentils, tamari or miso, salt, and pepper. Simmer another 10 minutes.

Serves 4

Almond Soup

1 cup raw almonds

1 cup milk

2 tablespoons butter

3 cups water

$1/4$ teaspoon salt

$1/4$ teaspoon Bell's seasoning or mixed ground turmeric, ground cumin, dried parsley, dried sage, dried rosemary, and dried thyme

$1/4$ cup non-fat plain yogurt

1. Puree almonds and milk together in a blender or food processor. Almonds will settle to bottom.

2. In a saucepan, simmer almond mixture until thickened, about 20 minutes.

3. Add all remaining ingredients except yogurt.

4. Remove from heat and whisk in yogurt.

Serves 4

Tomato Bisque

2 tablespoons butter

3 tablespoons flour

2 cups milk

2 cups tomato puree

I teaspoon dried basil

2 cups cooked brown rice

1/2 cup grated Parmesan cheese

Salt and pepper to taste

1. In a saucepan, melt butter over medium-low heat and whisk in flour. Stir for 3 minutes. Gradually stir in milk. Simmer until thickened.

2. Add tomato puree, basil, and brown rice. Simmer for 5 minutes.

3. Remove from heat. Stir in cheese, salt, and pepper.

Serves 4

Cream-of-Any-Vegetable Soup

This is one of my clean-the-fridge dishes (like minestrone and burgers). Sometimes I add fresh or dried herbs.

2 cups chopped vegetables
1 tablespoon butter
2 tablespoons whole-wheat flour
$1/2$ cup milk or soy milk or nut milk
Salt and pepper to taste

Optional Seasonings
Minced fresh dill with yellow vegetables or potatoes
Pinch of ground nutmeg with spinach, chard, or beet greens
Fresh or dried marjoram with zucchini, green beans, or tomatoes
Minced fresh parsley with cabbage, cauliflower, or broccoli

$1/2$ cup plain yogurt

1. Cook vegetables in salted boiling water to cover until tender. Drain.

2. In a blender, puree vegetables with milk.

3. In a small saucepan, melt butter over medium-low heat. Add flour and stir for 3 minutes. Gradually whisk in milk and cook until thickened.

4. Stir in vegetable puree, salt, and pepper and simmer 5 minutes.

5. Remove from heat and stir in optional seasoning and yogurt.

Serves 3

Mint Soup

A good cold soup to take to the beach in a cooler.

1 teaspoon cumin seeds

3 tablespoons sesame seeds

3 cups plain yogurt

2 cucumbers, peeled and chopped

1 tablespoon almond oil

$^1/_2$ teaspoon salt

3 tablespoons chopped fresh mint leaves (we like mild apple mint)

1. In a dry skillet toast seeds until light brown.

2. In a blender, grind seeds to a powder.

3. Add yogurt and cucumbers and puree.

4. Stir in oil, salt, and mint.

Serves 4

Cheddar Soup

This soup could also be a sauce. Alternatively, leave out the green peppers and add 3 cups chopped spinach at the end for a spinach-cheese sauce to dip strips of toast into.

 1 teaspoon butter
 1 cup finely chopped green bell pepper
 4 tablespoons flour
 5 cups milk
 3 cups shredded sharp Cheddar cheese
 Salt and pepper to taste
 Chopped fresh cilantro for garnish

1. Melt butter in a saucepan over medium heat and sauté bell peppers for about 8 minutes.

2. Sprinkle on the flour and gradually stir in milk.

3. Simmer for 5 minutes, stirring, then stir in cheese, salt, and pepper. Serve garnished with cilantro. Store in refrigerator for up to 5 days.

Tomato-Cheese Soup: Add 2 cups chopped fresh tomatoes or 1 cup tomato puree before adding cheese.

Makes about 5 cups; serves 4

Kale & Bean Curd Soup

I eat this soup nearly every day in the fall and winter, and often in the spring and summer. It is very soothing to the nerves (important if you're a fifth-grade teacher), and it is highly nutritious. I keep a carton of miso at school, so if I'm running late, I just grab a bunch of kale and a box of tofu as I run out the door. Only 5 minutes are needed to cook it up. This is a great soup!

    4 cups water
    1 pound extra-firm or firm tofu, cubed
    1 teaspoon sea salt
    4 cups chopped kale
    1 tablespoon yellow or white miso

1. In a soup pot, bring water to a boil. Add tofu, salt, and kale. Cook for 5 to 10 minutes.

2. Remove from heat and stir in miso.

Variations: Add potato peels to thicken. Add shredded carrots to boost vitamin A, or sprinkle liberally with sesame salt to boost calcium. Add grated ginger or dry mustard or both to help circulation. Replace kale with spinach, watercress, or chard.

Serves 2

Hotpot Soup

The first time I had this soup, it was brought to my table at a full boil with a flame under it. I extinguished the flame and waited a bit for it to cool down. In reality, this soup doesn't ever cool down, but it does clear out your sinuses.

2 small packages (8 ounces each) bean thread (cellophane) noodles

8 cups vegetable broth

$1/2$ teaspoon hing (asafetida)

2 tablespoons grated fresh ginger

2 tablespoons tamari sauce

1 tablespoons Asian sesame oil

$1/3$ cup red chili pepper puree

3 pounds firm tofu, drained and cut into $1/2$-inch dice

1 savoy cabbage, cored and shredded

1 bunch spinach, stemmed and chopped

1 fennel bulb, chopped

1 bunch watercress, stemmed and chopped

1 bunch broccoli, chopped

1. Break noodles into pieces.

2. In a soup pot, soak noodles in stock for 30 minutes.

3. Add all remaining ingredients and bring to a boil. Reduce heat to low and simmer for 30 minutes.

Serves 6

Tahini Soup

This is a simple, high-protein, high-calcium soup. Vegetables, tofu, or tempeh can be added to it.

> 6 cups vegetable broth
> I cup tahini
> Juice of I lemon
> I tablespoon chopped fresh cilantro

1. In a soup pot, bring broth to a boil and stir in tahini.

2. Add lemon juice and cilantro when serving.

Serves 6

Potato-Squash Soup

A hearty winter soup. We climbed Mt. Monadnock in the snow and found this a warming conclusion to our trek.

> 3 cups vegetable broth
> 2 medium butternut or buttercup squash, peeled and cubed (about 4 cups)
> 4 medium russet potatoes, peeled, and cubed (about 4 cups)
> I cup plain yogurt
> Lemon wedges for garnish

1. In a soup pot, bring broth to a boil.

2. Add squash and potatoes and cook until tender, about 25 minutes.

3. Remove from heat and stir in yogurt.

4. Puree in a blender until smooth. Serve with lemon wedges.

Serves 6

Savory Broths

These broths can be the base for barley, millet, rice, vegetable, or noodle soups. They may also be used to cook and marinate gluten or tofu. The brown and yellow broths can be made into gravy by whisking in about 3 tablespoons flour and simmering until thick.

Yellow Broth

5 cups water

1 teaspoon salt

$1/2$ teaspoon dried parsley

$1/2$ teaspoon dried sage

$1/2$ teaspoon dried thyme

$1/2$ teaspoon ground cumin

$1/2$ teaspoon ground turmeric

3 tablespoons nutritional yeast

1 tablespoon flax oil

1 tablespoon olive oil

1. In a saucepan, simmer water, salt, herbs, spices, and yeast together for 15 minutes.

2. Stir in flax oil and olive oil.

Makes about 5 cups

Brown Broth

5 cups water
$1/4$ cup tomato puree
$1/2$ cup tamari sauce
1 teaspoon salt
$1/2$ teaspoon dried parsley
Ground pepper to taste
1 tablespoon flax oil
1 tablespoon olive oil

1. In a saucepan, simmer water, tomato puree, tamari, salt, parsley, and pepper together for 15 minutes.

2. Stir in flax oil and olive oil.

Makes about 5 $3/4$ cups

Sea Broth

4 cups water
$1/4$ cup chopped dulse
1 teaspoon salt
Juice of 1 lemon
1 tablespoon molasses
$1/4$ teaspoon dried tarragon

In a saucepan, simmer all ingredients together for 15 minutes.

Makes about 4 cups

Vegetable Broth

2 carrots, peeled and chopped

3 stalks celery, chopped

$1/_2$ green bell pepper, seeded, deribbed, and chopped

2 tablespoons chopped fresh parsley

2 tablespoons tamari sauce

4 cups water

Salt to taste

1. Blend all ingredients in a blender or food processor.

2. In a saucepan, simmer for 35 minutes, or until vegetables are tender.

Makes about 6 cups

Scotch Broth

Pippi Longstocking thought barley was nasty. However, this is one of my kids' favorite cooked foods. I've seen them foraging in the fridge with friends after school, each with a spoon, eating it cold from the pot.

6 cups water

2 cups green split peas

1 turnip, diced

1 carrot, peeled and diced

1 cup fresh peas

1 cup pearl barley

$1/_4$ cup tamari sauce

1 teaspoon chopped fresh parsley

Salt and pepper to taste

2 tablespoons butter

Shredded Cheddar cheese for garnish (optional)

1. In a soup pot, bring water to a boil. Add split peas and vegetables. Reduce heat to low, cover, and simmer for 45 minutes.

2. Add barley and cook for 30 minutes. Stir to puree split peas. Add tamari, parsley, salt and pepper, and butter. Serve garnished with cheese, if you like.

Serves 6

Gravies

Nut Gravy

Use sparingly, as this is high in fat.

$1/4$ cup cashews
1 tablespoon hazelnuts
$1/2$ cup water
1 tablespoon butter
1 tablespoon flour
$1/8$ teaspoon salt

1. Grind nuts in a blender or food processor to a coarse flour; add water to blender and blend briefly.

2. In a small saucepan, melt butter over medium heat. Add flour and cook, stirring, to brown slightly.

3. Add nut mixture.

4. Add salt and stir until thickened.

Makes about $3/4$ cup

Dal Gravy

This is an interesting hot gravy to pour over cooked vegetables or grains. Thin it for soup or soup base, or mix it with yogurt, dried fruits, nuts, and chopped fresh vegetables to make an interesting salad.

> 2 cups yellow split peas
> 2 tablespoons salt
> 4 tablespoons curry powder

1. Soak peas overnight. In a saucepan, simmer peas for about 1 hour or until they squish when pressed between a finger and thumb.

2. Stir salt and curry powder into peas and simmer gently for 20 minutes. Taste and adjust seasoning. Add extra water to desired consistency.

Variations: In place of curry powder, use $1/4$ teaspoon hing (asafetida), 1 tablespoon ground turmeric, 2 tablespoons ground cumin, $1/2$ teaspoon ground coriander, pinch of cayenne powder, and 2 pinches mustard seed.

Makes 2 cups

Martha's Vegetable Broth Gravy

> 2 tablespoons butter
> 3 tablespoons whole-wheat flour
> 2 cups juice from cooked vegetables (carrots, celery, etc.)
> Salt to taste

In a saucepan, melt butter over medium heat. Whisk in flour and cook for 3 minutes. Gradually whisk in vegetable broth. Simmer until thickened. Add salt.

Makes 2 cups

Rotini in Red

This red sauce has a lot of carrot in it. The carrots can't be seen, but they cut the acid and sweeten the tomato sauce. They also add fiber and vitamin A. The rotini will remain hot in a thermos if the sauce is quite hot to start with.

    3 large carrots, peeled and finely grated
    3 cups tomato puree
    1 tablespoon minced fresh basil, or 2 teaspoons dried basil
    3 tablespoons olive oil
    2 tablespoons minced fresh marjoram, or 1 teaspoon dried marjoram
    1 pound rotini or penne pasta, cooked until al dente
    Grated Parmesan cheese to taste

1. In a saucepan, simmer carrots, tomato puree, basil, and marjoram for 1 hour. Stir in the olive oil.

2. Pour over pasta and add Parmesan cheese to taste.

Serves 4 to 6 depending upon appetite

Boston Baked Beans

    8 ounces firm tofu, diced
    1 cup shredded cabbage
    $1/_4$ cup canola oil
    3 cups dried navy beans or lima beans, soaked overnight and drained
    1 cup water
    $1/_2$ cup tomato puree
    1 tablespoon salt
    1 cup molasses
    2 tablespoons dry mustard

1. In a skillet, heat oil over medium heat and sauté cabbage and tofu until cabbage is tender, about 5 minutes.

2. Combine cabbage with all remaining ingredients in a baking dish. Cover and bake for 4 hours, or until tender. Add more liquid as needed.

Serves 6

Hearty Stew

2 carrots, peeled and chopped

4 potatoes, peeled and chopped

2 stalks celery, chopped

$1/2$ cup peas

2 cups chopped cabbage

$1/4$ cup canola oil

2 $1/2$ cups water, vegetable broth, or bean broth

2 cups cooked kidney beans

$1/4$ cup whole-wheat flour

$1/4$ cup tamari sauce

Salt and pepper to taste

1. In a saucepan, heat oil over medium heat and sauté vegetables for 5 minutes.

2. Add water or broth and simmer until tender, about 25 minutes.

3. Add all remaining ingredients and simmer 10 minutes more.

Serves 6

Brown Gluten Stew

This is made with Brown Gluten, also available in natural foods stores and often called *seitan*.

2 cups Brown Gluten (page 146) in 2 $1/2$ cups of its own broth
2 carrots, peeled and chopped
4 potatoes, peeled and chopped
2 stalks celery, chopped
$1/2$ cup peas
2 cups chopped cabbage
$1/4$ cup whole-wheat flour

1. In a saucepan, simmer gluten in gluten broth until firm, about 20 minutes.

2. Add vegetables. Simmer for 1 hour, or until tender.

3. Sprinkle flour over all and stir it in. Simmer 5 minutes more, or until thickened.

Serves 4

Thermos Foods

Rainbow Clouds

My children named this, originally because it was a different color each time I made it, depending on what vegetables I used. After the name, we started to try to put in as many colors of vegetables as we could. The beets stain, and my youngest poetically calls this "Pink Blossoms."

2 tablespoons butter

2 tablespoons flour

$1/_2$ cup milk or soy milk or nut milk

1 pound extra-firm or firm tofu, kneaded in a bowl for 2 minutes

2 cups corn kernels

1 cup grated carrots

1 cup chopped fresh spinach

1 cup chopped tomatoes or chopped cooked beets

Salt to taste

Grated cheese for garnish (optional)

1. In a saucepan, melt butter over medium-low heat. Add flour and stir for 3 minutes. Gradually whisk in milk and cook until thickened.

2. Stir in tofu and all vegetables except tomatoes or beets. Reduce heat to low, cover, and cook for 5 minutes.

3. Fold in tomatoes or beets and season with salt. Garnish with grated cheese, if you like.

Serves 4

Chili con Veg

2 tablespoons olive oil

2 cups chopped cabbage

2 cups corn kernels

1 zucchini, cubed

2 green bell peppers, seeded, deribbed, and chopped

3 cups cooked pinto or kidney beans

1 cup tomato sauce

$^1/_2$ cup texturized vegetable protein (TVP) or finely chopped Brown Gluten (page 146)

1 teaspoon chili powder (or more or less to taste), or pinch cayenne and 1 teaspoon ground cumin

Salt to taste

1. In a heavy pot over medium heat, heat oil and sauté vegetables for 5 to 8 minutes.

2. Add all remaining ingredients and simmer for 30 minutes, adding more liquid if needed.

Serves 4

Shepherd's Pie

This is a layered casserole that's always requested the next day for lunch thermoses. This is a favorite family food. It isn't beautiful or stylish, but simply delicious.

1. In a baking dish, make a layer of Tofu in Gravy (page 80).

2. Top with a layer of peas, then a layer of mashed potatoes.

3. Bake in a preheated 350°F oven for 20 minutes, or until hot and melded.

Cup-o-Lasagna

The amounts in this recipe depend on the size of your thermoses. Just keep layering until the thermos is full.

Flour tortillas
Tomato sauce
Shredded mozzarella or mild Cheddar cheese
Grated Parmesan cheese
Ricotta cheese
Fresh spinach leaves (optional)

1. Break tortillas into pieces the size of the thermos bottom.

2. Heat sauce very hot.

3. Layer tortillas, cheeses, sauce, and optional spinach, which will wilt nicely. Cap quickly, and by lunchtime, you'll have a warm, melty lasagna.

Sloppy Joes

Heat Chili con Veg (page 78) and pour into a thermos. At lunch, pour out onto a whole-wheat roll or English muffin.

Tofu in Gravy

This makes a good sauce to pour over noodles or send in a thermos to fill Bread Nests (page 20).

> 2 tablespoons butter
> 3 tablespoons whole-wheat flour
> 2 cups milk, vegetable broth, or nut milk
> 1 $1/2$ pounds firm tofu, drained and mashed or cubed
> $1/4$ cup tamari sauce

1. In a saucepan, melt butter over medium-low heat and whisk in flour. Stir for 3 minutes.

2. Gradually whisk in milk or broth and stir until thickened.

3. Add tofu and tamari and simmer gently for 5 minutes.

Makes about 4 cups; serves 4

Spicy Indian Vegetables

> 1 head cauliflower, chopped
> $1/2$ cup chopped cashews
> 1 cup cubed winter squash
> 1 tablespoon butter
> $1/4$ cup water or coconut milk
> $1/4$ teaspoon salt
> 2 cups chopped fresh spinach

1. In a saucepan, combine all ingredients except spinach. Bring to a boil, reduce heat to low, cover, and simmer gently for about 20 minutes.

2. Add more water or coconut milk, if necessary.

3. Stir in spinach at the end and cook a minute or two until wilted.

Serves 4

Curried Potatoes

3 tablespoons canola oil

$^1/_2$ teaspoon black mustard seeds

1 teaspoon ground cumin

1 $^1/_2$ teaspoons ground turmeric

$^1/_2$ teaspoon hing (asafetida)

$^1/_2$ teaspoon cayenne powder

1 teaspoon fennel seed

1 $^1/_2$ teaspoons salt

8 potatoes, peeled and cut into $^1/_2$-inch dice

1 cup water or coconut milk

1. In a saucepan, heat oil over medium heat and add mustard seeds. When they turn gray and start to jump, add remaining ingredients, stir, and cover.

2. Simmer until potatoes are done, about 20 minutes.

Serves 4

Spicy Mexican Vegetables

2 cups corn kernels

1 cup chopped green bell pepper

1 cup chopped red bell pepper

1 cup chopped cabbage

1 tablespoon canola oil

$1/3$ cup water

1 tablespoon chili powder

$1/4$ teaspoon salt

$1/2$ cup chopped black olives (optional)

1. In a saucepan, sauté vegetables in oil for 3 or 4 minutes.

2. Add water, chili powder, and salt.

3. Bring to a boil, reduce heat to low, cover, and simmer gently for about 15 minutes, adding water if necessary. When done cooking, stir in olives.

Serves 4

Calcium Drink

I invented this drink when I was a nursing mother allergic to milk. The children started begging sips, and now it runs a close third behind hot chocolate or hot cinnamon milk for a winter warm-up drink.

> 4 cups cold water
> $1/2$ cup old-fashioned rolled oats
> Pinch of salt
> Pinch of fennel seeds
> $1/2$ cup sunflower seeds
> 2 to 4 tablespoons honey, or to taste

1. In a saucepan, simmer water, oats, salt, and fennel seeds for 20 minutes.

2. Process all ingredients in a blender and drink warm. Shake thermos before drinking to stir up the sunflower seeds.

Serves 4

CHAPTER 4

Salads & Salad Dressings

Chapter Contents

CHAPTER 4

Salads
&
Salad
Dressings

Salads are getting more difficult to identify these days. Usually, though, they are served cold, with a dressing and at least one raw ingredient. From there, anything goes.

Try cooked vegetables, marinated vegetables, raw vegetables, potatoes, pasta, grains, beans, sprouts, cheeses, fruits and tofu. Jellied salads are fun to make, pretty to look at, and delicious. Raw foods are one of the most important components of a healthful diet, so salads deserve some attention, creativity, and plenty of space at every meal.

Many of the recipes in this chapter do not include exact amounts; you may vary these according to your taste and what you have on hand.

Carrot Salad

2 cups grated carrots

$1/2$ cup raisins

I cup plain yogurt or Tofu Mayonnaise (page 164), or a combination

Stir all ingredients together.

Serves 4

Coleslaw

I cup Tofu Mayonnaise (page 164) or a non-fat plain yogurt and Tofu
   Mayonnaise combination

3 cups grated cabbage

$1/2$ cups grated carrot (optional)

I cup raisins or chopped pineapple (optional)

1. Add the dressing to the grated cabbage.

2. If desired, stir in grated carrot, raisins, and/or pineapple.

Serves 2 to 4

Brussels Sprouts Salad

3 cups steamed small Brussels sprouts, cooled

2 cups chopped apples

2 cups chopped chestnuts

$1/2$ cup Tofu Mayonnaise (page 164) or Nut Milk Mayonnaise (page 163)

In a bowl, stir all ingredients together.

Serves 6

Potato & Miscellaneous Salad

Other ingredients to add to this salad include $1/2$ to 1 cup cooked beans or chick-peas, raw green beans or peas, $1/2$ cup toasted sunflower seeds, or bean sprouts.

6 potatoes, peeled, boiled, and cubed

10 black or green olives

$1/4$ cup chopped pickles (any kind you like)

3 stalks celery, chopped

$1/3$ cup chopped bell pepper

1 tablespoon salt (less if pickles are salty or if you use green olives)

2 teaspoons cider vinegar

1 $1/2$ cups plain yogurt

In a bowl, mix all ingredients together. Let sit at least 3 hours to blend flavors.

Variation: Replace $1/2$ cup of yogurt with $1/2$ cup French Dressing (page 107). Marinate salad overnight.

Serves 8

Curried Potato Salad

Curried Potatoes (page 81), cooled
1 green bell pepper, seeded, deribbed, and chopped
$1/_2$ cup chopped celery
$1/_2$ cup plain yogurt

In a bowl, fold together all ingredients and let stand for at least 4 hours.

Serves 6

Green Bean & Feta Salad

2 cups green beans, trimmed
3 tablespoons Thyme Vinaigrette (page 110)
$1/_4$ cup crumbled feta cheese

1. Steam green beans over boiling water in a covered pot until emerald green, about 10 minutes. Drain.

2. Place beans in a bowl and pour vinaigrette over them. Let cool. Top with feta cheese.

3. Toss and refrigerate for at least 1 hour or overnight.

Serves 2

Guacamole Salad

2 large avocados, peeled, pitted, and cubed

2 large tomatoes, cubed

2 tablespoons fresh lemon juice

I teaspoon chopped fresh parsley

Pinch of chili powder

Salt and pepper to taste

In a bowl, fold all ingredients together and refrigerate. Can be slightly mashed and eaten on toasted tortilla chips.

Serves 4

Linguine Salad

4 ounces linguine, broken into thirds and cooked until al dente

20 black olives, pitted and coarsely chopped

$^1/_2$ recipe Mama Papa's Peppers (page 92)

I teaspoon snipped fresh basil

4 tomatoes, finely chopped

Salt to taste

Olive oil to taste

In a bowl, fold all ingredients together. Adjust seasoning to taste.

Serves 4

Mama Papa's Peppers

Mrs. Papa was my sister's Italian grandmother-in-law. She made these for all their family gatherings. These are good alone or in a salad.

4 red bell peppers
2 tablespoons olive oil
$^3/_4$ teaspoon salt

1. Roast peppers in a preheated 400°F oven for 25 minutes, turning once.

2. Peel and seed peppers and cut into long strips.

3. In a bowl, mix with oil and salt. Marinate overnight.

Marinated Vegetables

Steam vegetables (Sliced peeled beets, green beans, wax beans, sliced peeled carrots, sliced peeled potatoes, broccoli, or cauliflower florets) until crisp-tender. Green ones should be brilliant green. Marinate in Thyme Vinaigrette (page 110) or Herb Vinegar (page 108) for at least 24 hours. Add salt to taste, if desired.

Pastafazool

1 cup cooked kidney beans
3 cups fusilli, cooked until al dente
3 tablespoons olive oil
3 tablespoons red wine vinegar

In a bowl, stir all ingredients together. Marinate in refrigerator overnight.

Soy-Tomato Aspic

My grandmother used to make this often. I've replaced the gelatin she used (non-vegetarian) with agar agar, which works just as well. This is good with Tofu Mayonnaise (page 164).

$1/2$ teaspoon chopped fresh basil or dill
$1/2$ teaspoon chopped fresh parsley
8 ounces firm tofu, drained and kneaded until evenly crumbled
$1/4$ cup finely chopped bell pepper
1 cup tomato juice or V8
$1/4$ teaspoon fresh lemon juice
1 tablespoon tamari sauce
$1/2$ tablespoon granulated agar agar

1. In a bowl, mix herbs, tofu, and peppers together; set aside.

2. Combine liquids and agar agar in a saucepan and let sit for a few minutes.

3. Bring to a boil, stirring constantly, and cook, stirring, for 3 minutes.

4. Let cool. Stir in herb mixture. Pour into a 2-cup mold and refrigerate until set, about 1 hour.

Serves 4

Taboulleh

3 cups cooked bulgur

$3/4$ cup Italian dressing (try a low-fat type)

$1/3$ cup chopped celery

$1/3$ cup chopped green or red bell pepper

$1/2$ cup chopped fresh parsley

In a bowl, mix all ingredients together. Marinate overnight.

Serves 4

Three-to-Five Bean Salad

2 tablespoons honey

2 teaspoons tamari sauce

1 tablespoon canola oil

1 tablespoon red wine vinegar

1 cup cooked chickpeas

1 cup cooked green beans, cut 1-inch long

1 cup cooked kidney beans and/or wax and lima beans

1. In a bowl, combine honey, tamari, oil, and vinegar. Pour over beans.

2. Stir beans gently and refrigerate for 24 hours.

Serves 5

Vinegared Beets

Mix these with some cottage cheese and eat on lettuce for a quick summer lunch.

3 cups diced cooked beets
1 cup reserved beet cooking liquid
$1/4$ cup cider vinegar

In a bowl, combine all ingredients. Marinate overnight in beet-cooking water and vinegar (ratio of 1 to 1).

Serves 3

Waldorf Salad

$1/2$ cup raisins
$1/2$ cup chopped celery
1 cup chopped apples
1 cup Nut Milk Mayonnaise (page 163)

In a bowl, stir all ingredients together. Refrigerate.

Serves 4

Ginger & Chickpea Salad

This nutritious salad gives you all the digestive and circulatory benefits enhanced by ginger. In India, this is a breakfast food. These are chickpeas brought to the edge of sprouting. A breakfast full of vitality. I think it beats oatmeal when the weather is hot, but then, I like cold pizza or Greek salad in the morning, too.

    4 to 5 tablespoons thinly slivered or shredded fresh ginger
    Juice of $^1/_2$ lemon
    1 cup chickpeas

Soak chickpeas overnight. Drain and rinse in the morning. Rinse a second time that evening, and a final time the following morning. Sprinkle ginger over chickpeas. Squeeze lemon juice over all.

Serves 3

Winter Solstice Salad

New Hampshire winters go on for a bit. We need to carry a little summer in our hearts and in our pantries to make it through without heading for the Virgin Islands. I always plant yellow and red cherry tomatoes in preparation. They go in the flower garden or in pots near the door, so that the children can snack. When the tomatoes get ahead of us, I cut them in halves and dehydrate them. Stored in glass jars, they keep all winter and remind us that there is really a time when it is warm enough for tomatoes to grow.

  1 pound penne or rotini pasta
  1 cup dry-packed sun-dried tomatoes
  2 green bell peppers, roasted, peeled, seeded, deribbed, and sliced
  1 can water-packed artichoke hearts, drained and quartered
  2 cups black olives, pitted and chopped
  2 cups cooked chickpeas (optional)
  4 tablespoons olive oil
  Juice of $^1/_2$ lemon
  2 tablespoons minced fresh herbs of choice

1. Cook pasta in salted boiling water until al dente.

2. Add the sun-dried tomatoes to water with pasta. Drain.

3. Add all remaining ingredients and mix.

Serves 6

Greek Pasta Salad

This isn't the least bit authentic, but another salad with ingredients that are available in winter.

16 ounces small shell pasta
1 cup black olives, pitted and chopped
1 cup green olives, pitted and chopped
$1/2$ cup crumbled feta cheese
4 cups shredded fresh spinach leaves
1 tablespoon snipped fresh chives
$1/4$ cup olive oil
Juice of $1/2$ lemon
$1/2$ cup sliced roasted peppers

1. Cook the pasta in salted boiling water until al dente. Drain.

2. Assemble all remaining ingredients in a large bowl and pour pasta on top. Mix well. Spinach will wilt.

Serves 8

Asian Noodle Salad

This salad is a perennial favorite at the High Mowing School May Day Festival. Though Asian Noodle Salad and a May Day Festival seem incongruous, together they have become a lovely tradition.

$1/_4$ cup water

2 tablespoons tamari sauce

3 tablespoons tahini

2 tablespoons rice vinegar

1 tablespoon molasses

1 teaspoon chili oil

2 teaspoons Asian sesame oil

8 ounces linguine noodles, broken in thirds

1 tablespoon chopped fresh cilantro

2 tablespoons chopped fresh chives

1. In a saucepan, heat water and add tamari, tahini, vinegar, molasses, and oils. Mix well and set aside.

2. Cook noodles until tender. Drain.

3. Stir in sauce. Top with herbs.

Serves 6

Matchstick Salad

All the ingredients in this Asian inspired salad are readily available in winter in the Northeast.

3 cups vegetable broth
1 cup matchstick-cut carrots
1 cup matchstick-cut red bell peppers
1 cup matchstick-cut celery
4 squares aromatic dried tofu (available in Asian markets)

Dressing
1 tablespoon tamari sauce
1 teaspoon rice vinegar
1 tablespoon peanut butter
$1/4$ teaspoon chili oil
2 teaspoons Asian sesame oil
Pinch salt
1 teaspoon molasses
1 teaspoon dry sherry

1. In a saucepan, bring broth to a boil. Add vegetables and tofu. Cook for 30 seconds. Drain (reserve broth for another soup).

2. Combine dressing ingredients and pour over vegetables.

Serves 4

Beet & Potato Salad

A good salad to make in the fall when the beets and new potatoes are harvested, and the cucumbers haven't yet been thrown in the pickle crock.

    6 cups cubed peeled potatoes, cooked until almost tender
    2 cups cubed peeled beets, cooked
    I cup cubed cucumber
    2 cups plain yogurt
    2 tablespoons olive oil, or I teaspoon flaxseed oil
    2 tablespoons snipped fresh chives

In a bowl, gently stir all ingredients together.

Serves 8

Chestnut Salad

Another fall salad, this one is sort of a Greek Waldorf salad.

    I pear, peeled, cored, and chopped
    I apple, peeled, cored, and chopped
    $^1/_2$ cup peeled cooked chestnuts, quartered
    $^1/_2$ cup chopped celery
    I tablespoon balsamic vinegar
    2 tablespoons olive oil
    I tablespoon minced fresh parsley
    I tablespoon crumbled feta cheese

In a bowl, combine all ingredients and stir to mix.

Serves 3

Vegetarian Chicken Salad

My mother-in-law says that I don't remember what a chicken tastes like, but my father-in-law, who smokes, is fooled every time.

     1 package dried tofu skin, broken into bite-sized pieces
     2 cups chopped celery
     1 cup Tofu Mayonnaise (page 164)

1. Cook tofu skin in boiling water for 10 minutes. Drain and let cool.

2. Stir in celery and mayonnaise.

Serves 4

Artichoke Salad Cups

An artichoke is a beautiful vegetable. When steamed and filled it sits on a plate like an unfolding water lily. However, artichokes sometimes have little thorn-like points on the tips of their leaves. These prickly tips can be cut off by truncating the top $1/2$-inch of the whole artichoke. Steam for 50 minutes, or cook for 10 minutes in a pressure cooker. Gently pull back leaves enough to pull out inner white thin leaves. Remove choke with a teaspoon. Fill with Tofu Salad (page 44), Ginger & Chickpea Salad (page 96), Hummus (page 35), or Guacamole (page 91).

Salad in Vegetable Cups

2 tablespoons olive oil

2 tablespoons wine or balsamic vinegar

Salt and pepper to taste

1 tablespoon chopped fresh dill, marjoram, chives, or basil

1 cup shredded Swiss cheese

1 cup shredded mild Cheddar cheese

2 cups cooked brown rice

6 bell peppers or tomatoes

Croutons for topping

1. Combine oil, vinegar, salt, pepper, and herbs.

2. Mix with cheeses and rice. Set aside for 15 minutes while preparing vegetable cups.

3. Cut off tops of vegetables and scoop out seeds and ribs of peppers and flesh of tomatoes. Tops may be replaced for travel.

4. Pack in cheese mixture and top with a few croutons.

Variations: Stuff bell peppers with potato salad or other fillings. Stuff tomatoes with Hummus (page 35), or Linguine Salad (page 91) without the tomato in it.

Serves 6

Turtles-in-the-Mud Salad

This recipe started out as a joke, which was enjoyed and became a regular. This doesn't look like a traveling salad, but the kids like to bring the components to school to assemble before their friends.

Turtles
$1/2$ cup water
$1/2$ teaspoon granulated agar agar
2 tablespoons fresh lemon juice
1 $1/4$ cup cooked lima beans, pureed
$1/2$ cup finely chopped spinach
2 tablespoons minced fresh dill
$1/2$ teaspoon salt

Mud
$1/2$ cup mayonnaise or Tofu Mayonnaise (page 164)
1 tablespoon miso

$1/4$ cup cashew halves
3 olives cut into O's (to decorate the turtles' back)

1. To make turtles: In a saucepan, mix water and agar agar together. Let sit for 2 minutes.

2. Bring to a boil and cook for 2 minutes, stirring. Let cool.

3. Stir in lemon juice, lima bean puree, spinach, dill, and salt.

4. Refrigerate until set, about 2 hours.

5. Using a tablespoon, scoop out 4 oval shapes for turtle shells. These will stay solid at room temperature, but they water a bit overnight (just drain it off).

6. To make the mud: Mash the miso with a fork until softened.

7. Add the mayonnaise a little at a time.

8. Set the turtles into the mud. Give them a head, tail, and feet of cashews and decorate their back with olive O's.

Serves 4

Dressings

Blue Cheese Dressing

1 cup cottage cheese
$1/4$ cup plain yogurt
3 tablespoons blue cheese
Pinch of salt

Blend all ingredients together in a blender until smooth. Store in a covered jar in the refrigerator for up to 1 week.

Makes about 1 $1/4$ cups

Creamy Blue Cheese Dressing

1 $1/2$ cups Yogurt Cheese (page 51)
2 tablespoons crumbled blue cheese

In a bowl, stir Yogurt Cheese and blue cheese together. Store in a covered jar in the refrigerator for up to 1 week.

Makes 1 $1/2$ cups

Tomato Vinaigrette

$1/2$ tablespoon flaxseed oil (a good source for essential fatty acids)
2 tablespoons olive oil
1 cup chopped tomato
1 teaspoon Dijon mustard
2 tablespoons balsamic vinegar
1 teaspoon each, fresh basil and marjoram

Put all ingredients into a blender and blend until smooth. Store in a covered jar or bottle in the refrigerator for up to 1 week.

Makes 1 $1/2$ cups

Creamy Cucumber Dressing

1 cucumber, peeled and finely chopped
1 cup plain yogurt
Pinch of salt
3 tablespoons minced fresh dill

In a bowl, stir all ingredients together. Store in a covered jar in the refrigerator for up to 3 days.

French Dressing

2 tablespoons honey
4 tablespoons cider vinegar
1 teaspoon paprika
1 teaspoon salt
2 tablespoons olive oil
$1/4$ cup plain yogurt
1 cup Yogurt Cheese (Page 51)

In a bowl, combine all ingredients and stir until blended. Store in a covered jar in the refrigerator for up to 5 days.

Makes 1 $1/2$ cups

Herb-Cheese Dressing

$1/_2$ cup minced fresh parsley, thyme, dill or basil, or 1/4 cup minced fresh
   tarragon
I cup cottage cheese
I cup plain yogurt
Pinch or two of salt

Process all ingredients together in a blender until smooth. Store in a covered jar in the refrigerator for up to I week.

Makes 2 cups

Herb Vinegars

Put a few tablespoons of a minced fresh herb in a jar. Bring vinegar to a boil and pour over herb. Let sit overnight. Strain out herb and discard. Pour vinegar into a bottle and place a sprig of whole herb in it. Ready to use. To store, set in a cool dark place.

Or, combine herbs and unheated vinegar in a bottle. Set in a sunny window for 2 weeks, shaking daily. Store in a cool dark place.

Note: Purple basil makes pink vinegar.

Russian Dressing

1 cup Tofu Mayonnaise (page 164)

$^1/_4$ cup ketchup

2 tablespoons pickle relish

1 teaspoon cider vinegar

1 teaspoon paprika

Pinch of salt

Pinch of wasabi powder

In a bowl, stir all ingredients together. Keep in a covered jar in the refrigerator for up to 1 week.

Makes 1 $^1/_4$ cups

Linda's House Dressing

$^1/_4$ cup balsamic vinegar

Juice of $^1/_2$ lemon (optional)

3 tablespoons tamari sauce

$^1/_4$ cup olive oil

1 tablespoon flaxseed oil

$^1/_4$ teaspoon minced fresh thyme

$^1/_4$ teaspoon minced fresh basil (if it isn't already in the salad)

$^1/_4$ teaspoon minced fresh marjoram

In a bowl, stir all ingredients together. Keep in a covered bottle or jar in the refrigerator for up to 5 days.

Makes $^3/_4$ cup

Thyme Vinaigrette

3 tablespoons red wine vinegar

1 large ripe red tomato, chopped

$3/4$ teaspoon Dijon mustard

1 $1/2$ teaspoons chopped fresh thyme

Tiny pinch of freshly ground black pepper

Blend all ingredients together in a blender until smooth. Keep in a covered jar in the refrigerator for up to 1 week.

Makes 1 cup

CHAPTER 5

Main Dishes

Chapter Contents

CHAPTER 5

Main
Dishes

Most of the following recipes are dishes I usually make for dinner. Leftovers are for lunch. Sometimes a dinner is so well liked that I have to double the portions so I can make lunches the next day (it's a policy at our house that I only cook once a day).

Many of these foods are nice to dip into a sauce that is separately packaged. Besides workday lunch-box items, they are great on picnics, on car trips, or for ski trip lunches. They aren't generally messy, all will hold their shape and are good hot or cold.

Eggplant Rolls

These taste fine cold, or you can box up the eggplant rolls and put the hot tomato sauce in a thermos.

I globe eggplant, cut into eight $^1/_4$-inch-thick slices
Salt for sprinkling
2 tablespoons olive oil
I cup ricotta cheese
3 tablespoons grated Parmesan cheese
2 tablespoons chopped fresh basil or marjoram
2 cups tomato sauce

1. Sprinkle each slice of eggplant with salt and let sit for 30 minutes.

2. Brush moisture and salt off. Brush olive oil on each side of each slice. Place on a baking sheet and bake in a preheated 350°F oven for 20 minutes.

3. In a bowl, stir cheeses and herbs together.

4. Spread each slice with filling, roll up, and tie with string or secure with a toothpick.

5. Pour tomato sauce over rolls and bake in a preheated 350°F oven for 30 minutes, or until heated throughout and melty.

Makes 8 rolls; serves 4

Cabbage Rolls

These are good dipped in a thermos of hot Tomato Bisque Soup (page 62).

I large cabbage
2 cups cooked rice
I cup cottage cheese
3 tablespoons minced fresh basil, dill, or thyme

1. Drop whole, cored cabbage into boiling water and simmer until leaves are soft enough to be peeled off, about 10 minutes once water has returned to a boil

2. Separate leaves and let cool to touch.

3. In a bowl, stir rice, cottage cheese, and herbs together.

4. Place about 3 tablespoons filling in center of 8 leaves and roll up, folding in edges as you roll. Tie with a string or hold together with a toothpick for travel. Alternatively, roll up cigar fashion.

Makes 8 rolls; serves 4

Kohlrabi Cups

3 kohlrabi

1 cup finely chopped cabbage

1 tablespoon butter

1 cup Soy Scrapple (page 132)

4 ounces firm tofu, drained and mashed

$1/2$ cup Yogurt Cheese (page 51)

2 tablespoons walnuts, ground in a blender

1. Peel kohlrabi and steam over boiling water in a covered pot for 20 minutes, or until tender.

2. Scoop out centers, leaving $1/2$-inch-thick walls.

3. In a saucepan, melt butter over medium heat and sauté cabbage until it wilts.

4. Add Soy Scrapple and tofu. Stir in yogurt cheese.

5. Fill cups with tofu mixture. Top with walnuts.

6. Place in an oiled pan. Bake in a preheated 400°F oven for 10 to 20 minutes, or until all flavors blend.

Serves 3

Spiced Stuffed Peppers

1 cup Soy Scrapple (page 132)
$^1/_2$ cup plain yogurt
1 $^1/_4$ pounds extra-firm or firm tofu
1 teaspoon chopped fresh basil
1 $^1/_2$ teaspoons salt
$^1/_2$ cup chopped almonds
2 to 3 cups tomato sauce
6 green bell peppers

1. Mix together all ingredients except tomato sauce and peppers.

2. Cut off tops of peppers and scoop out seeds.

3. Stuff with mixture. Place in a deep baking dish.

4. Pour tomato sauce over all, cover with aluminum foil or a cover, and bake in a pre-heated 350°F oven for 45 minutes, or until hot and lightly browned.

Serves 6

Potpies

I usually make a large potpie in a Dutch oven to spoon into thermoses, but individual ones can go to the office to be heated in an oven or microwave. Alternatively, you can use puff pastry or pie crust, make individual turnovers, or simply send one of the Bread Nests (page 20) to fill.

For a quick method, put cubed tofu in a casserole and add a bag of frozen mixed vegetables. Pour a white sauce over all and cover with a few filo leaves sprayed with oil. Bake until bubbly and crusty. I make my potpies in a rustic style, so I don't peel anything unless it isn't organically grown.

Filling
1 cup water
3 potatoes, $1/_2$-inch cubed
1 carrot, $1/_2$-inch cubed
2 cups peas
1 cup chopped turnips, $1/_2$-inch cubed
1 pound firm tofu, drained
2 tablespoons butter
2 tablespoons flour
2 cups milk
Salt and pepper to taste

Dumpling Crust
$1/_2$ cup unbleached white or white whole-wheat or whole-wheat pastry
    flour
$1/_2$ cup water
$1/_4$ cup Yogurt Cheese (page 51)
$1/_2$ teaspoon baking soda
$1/_4$ teaspoon salt
1 tablespoon honey

1. In a saucepan, bring water to a boil. Add vegetables and tofu, reduce heat, and simmer until vegetables are tender, about 15 to 20 minutes. Set aside.

2. In another saucepan, melt butter over medium heat. Whisk in flour and stir for 3 minutes. Gradually whisk in milk. Simmer, stirring, until thickened.

3. Add white sauce to tofu and vegetables.

4. Pour into a casserole dish.

5. Stir all crust ingredients together.

6. Scoop out large spoonfuls of dumpling dough and pat to flatten slightly.

7. Drop each dumpling on top of filling. Dumplings should cover the top of filling with their edges touching.

8. Bake in a preheated 350°F oven until browned and bubbly, about 15 minutes.

Serves 6

Asparagus in a Cast

6 pieces sliced bread, crusts removed

3 tablespoons Tofu Mayonnaise (page 164)

6 cooked asparagus stalks

1 tablespoon butter, melted

1. Flatten bread with a rolling pin and spread with mayonnaise.

2. Place asparagus on bread with a little sticking out of each end. Roll bread up.

3. Brush with butter and bake, seam-side down, in a preheated 375°F oven for about 15 minutes, or until lightly crusty.

Serves 3

Welsh Rarebit

I'm not sure of the authenticity of this recipe, but it's what my family has always called Welsh Rarebit. This is not low in fat.

3 tablespoons butter

3 tablespoons whole-wheat flour

1 cup nonfat milk

1 cup shredded sharp Cheddar cheese

$1/2$ teaspoon dry mustard

1. Melt butter in a saucepan over medium heat. Add flour and stir to brown lightly over low heat.

2. Gradually add milk, stirring constantly, until thickened.

3. Add cheese and mustard. Heat until the cheese melts. Stir to blend.

4. Serve over toast or biscuits.

Serves 4

Golden Tofu Nuggets

This is one of only three fried foods in this book. My children insisted that Tofu Nuggets couldn't be left out.

> $1/_4$ cup nutritional yeast
> $1/_4$ cup arrowroot or cornstarch
> 1 pound extra-firm or firm tofu, drained
> Salt to taste
> Canola oil for frying

1. Set tofu on a cutting board that is slightly tilted to allow water to drain away. Put a plate or some sort of flat weight on it. Let sit draining for 30 minutes to 1 hour.

2. Cut tofu into $3/_4$-inch cubes.

3. In a heavy plastic bag, mix nutritional yeast, arrowroot or cornstarch, and salt. Add tofu cubes and shake until coated.

4. In a heavy skillet, heat $1/_2$-inch oil until hot, but not smoking. Drop cubes into hot oil. Cook for 3 minutes, or until golden. Turn and cook for 3 minutes, or until golden.

5. Using a slotted spoon, transfer to paper towels to drain. Serve with Tofu Tartar Sauce (page 172) or Spicy Tofu Mayonnaise (page 164).

Serves 4

Somewhat Knishes

Fill with your choice of fillings from this book. Since the fillings aren't traditional, my knish-eating friend named them somewhat knishes.

> $1/2$ cup mashed potatoes
> 1 $1/2$ cups whole-wheat pastry flour
> $1/2$ teaspoon salt
> $1/2$ teaspoon baking powder
> 1 tablespoon canola oil
> $1/3$ cup water
> Filling of choice

1. In a bowl, knead all ingredients except filling together. Let sit for 30 minutes.

2. On a floured board, roll mixture out very thin and cut into 4- x 5-inch rectangles.

3. Place filling in center of each rectangle. Fold corners in and seal.

4. Place, seam-side down, on an oiled baking sheet. Spray with vegetable-oil cooking spray and bake at in a preheated 350°F oven for 30 minutes, or until golden.

Serves 6

Polenta

Bake, fry, or eat this as is, with Spicy Mexican Vegetables (page 82) or Refried Bean Spread (page 38) and a dollop of yogurt.

> 5 cups water
> I teaspoon salt
> I cup cornmeal (coarsely ground)

1. Combine all ingredients in a saucepan.

2. Whisk out lumps. Cook over medium-heat stirring constantly until thickened and pulls away from pan sides when stirring, about 30 to 40 minutes. Pour into an oiled pan or dish. Let cool. Slide it out of pan and slice.

Cheese Polenta: Just before pouring cornmeal mixture into pan or dish, stir in $1/2$ cup shredded Cheddar cheese and $1/2$ cup shredded Parmesan cheese.

Spicy Polenta: Add 2 teaspoons ground cumin and $1/4$ teaspoon cayenne pepper while cooking polenta.

Serves 6

Italian Cereal Squares

I invented this when I was pregnant and needed to eat within 10 minutes of rising or succumb to morning sickness. You may want to send along grated Parmesan cheese to sprinkle on these for lunch.

> 1 cup water
> $^1/_2$ cup uncooked cream of wheat (farina)
> $^1/_2$ cup chopped vegetables (bell peppers, bean sprouts, cabbage)
> 1 cup tomato sauce
> 1 cup shredded mozzarella and Cheddar cheese
> Salt to taste

1. In a saucepan, bring water to a boil.

2. Stir cereal and vegetables into boiling water. Reduce heat and simmer for 3 minutes.

3. Add tomato sauce and salt. Cook to a slightly sticky consistency, about 5 more minutes.

4. Quickly stir in cheese and pour into an 8- x 8-inch square pan. Let cool slightly, then cut into squares.

5. Eat plain or dip into more tomato sauce at lunchtime.

Serves 4

Chickpea Soufflé

2 cups dried soybeans, soaked overnight or 10 to 12 hours and drained

2 $1/2$ cups water

$1/2$ teaspoon ground turmeric

$1/2$ teaspoon dried thyme

$1/4$ teaspoon hing (asafetida)

$1/2$ teaspoon dried sage

$1/2$ teaspoon dried parsley

2 teaspoons salt

2 tablespoons nutritional yeast

2 tablespoons pine nuts (optional)

$1/3$ cup chickpea flour (grind dried chickpeas in a blender or food processor)

$1/4$ cup canola oil

Cranberry Ketchup (page 159), for serving

1. Process soybeans, water, spices, herbs, salt, yeast, and nuts in blender or food processor.

2. With motor running, gradually add chickpea flour, then oil.

3. Pour into a casserole dish and bake for 15 minutes in a preheated 350°F oven. Reduce heat to 300°F and cook for 1 $1/2$ hours.

4. Let cool and eat with Cranberry Ketchup.

Serves 4

Stuffed Tofu Triangles

3 cups chopped spinach
1 cup shredded Cheddar cheese
Salt to taste
1 pound firm tofu, drained
4 tablespoons canola oil
Goma-shio for sprinkling

1. Steam spinach over boiling water in a covered pot until it wilts. In a bowl, combine spinach with cheese and salt. Cover and set aside.

2. Slice tofu into 1-inch-thick slabs; press gently to drain.

3. Heat oil in a skillet over medium heat.

4. Fry tofu in hot oil until golden brown.

5. Cut each square of tofu in half diagonally. Cut out middle of each triangle to make a pocket, leaving a $1/4$-inch-thick wall.

6. Gently press spinach-cheese stuffing inside each triangle. Sprinkle goma-shio on surface.

Makes 8 triangles; serves 4

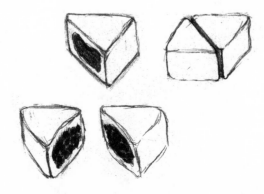

Baked Stuffed Tomatoes

I like these cold, with a squeeze of lemon on them.

2 large tomatoes
2 tablespoons butter
1 cup fresh bread crumbs
Pinch of black pepper
Pinch of salt
1 tablespoon minced fresh parsley
$1/4$ teaspoon dried thyme
$1/4$ teaspoon dried marjoram
2 tablespoons grated Parmesan cheese

1. Cut tomatoes in half and scoop out insides. Chop insides.

2. Place chopped tomato and other ingredients in a skillet. Over medium heat, stir together until the butter melts. Stir in cheese.

3. Stuff into tomato shells and bake in a preheated 350°F oven for 20 to 30 minutes, or until golden brown on top. Eat hot or cold.

Serves 2

Skillet Potatoes

These are loved by children, but they are not low in fat.

1 teaspoon canola oil, plus 2 to 4 tablespoons canola oil for frying
$1/3$ cup shredded cabbage
3 cups finely diced cold cooked potatoes
1/4 teaspoon salt
Pinch of pepper
3 tablespoons flour
$1/4$ cup milk, soy milk, or nut milk

1. In a small skillet, heat 1 teaspoon oil over medium heat and sauté cabbage until soft.

2. In a bowl, mix cabbage and all remaining ingredients except remaining oil.

3. In a skillet, heat 2 to 4 tablespoons oil over low heat. Pack potato mixture into a pan. Cook until golden, flip, and cook other side. Cut into wedges, like a pie.

Serves 4

Jeweled Yuba Logs

I green bell pepper

I ripe tomato

I cucumber, cut into quarters lengthwise and then cut to length of yuba
sheets

3 sheets yuba, steamed for I minute to soften

Tofu Mayonnaise (page 164) for serving

1. Cut off tops of pepper and tomato and scoop out seeds and insides.

2. Cut pepper and tomato around and around the vegetable to form a continuous strip
$1/4$- to $1/2$-inch wide. Cut to same length as cucumber, so that all vegetable strips are
same length as yuba sheets.

3. Arrange one third of each vegetable in a bundle in center of each yuba sheet. Roll
into a log shape.

4. Roll in waxed paper and twist the ends. Cut into circles about I-inch thick and serve
with a dollop of mayonnaise.

Makes 3 logs; serves 3

Potato Griddlecakes

These cakes are good hot or cold. Try them with thermos-held hot Cream-of-Any-Vegetable Soup (page 63) spooned over them, or spread with apple butter.

I cup hot water (warm to the touch, about 100°F)
I teaspoon cornstarch
4 ounces firm or extra-firm tofu
I tablespoon active dry yeast (packages contain I tablespoon each)
$^3/_4$ cup whole-wheat flour
I cup grated raw potatoes
I teaspoon salt

1. Combine water, cornstarch, and tofu in a blender or food processor. Puree until smooth.

2. Pour puree into a bowl and add yeast. Let sit for 5 minutes, or until foamy.

3. Stir in flour, potatoes, and salt. Beat well with wooden spoon.

4. Let rise in a warm place for 30 minutes. Beat again. Heat a well-greased griddle or skillet over medium heat. Pour out $^1/_3$-cup portions. Turn when browned and cook on other side.

Serves 4

Crusty Bread Loaf

Fun for a picnic, or make into crusty rolls for individual lunches. Send along a container of sauce or mayonnaise.

    1 loaf Italian bread
    2 tablespoons butter at room temperature for spreading
    Soy Scrapple (page 132), Vermont Nut Loaf (page 144), or ground Brown
        Gluten (page 146) for filling

1. Cut off one end of bread and scoop out the insides, leaving a $1/_2$-inch layer all around.

2. Butter inside to keep bread from getting soggy, and pack filling tightly into cavity.

3. Wrap and refrigerate for 2 or 3 hours.

4. Cut into 1-inch-thick diagonal slices to serve.

Serves 6

Soy Scrapple

Soy scrapple can be used, without frying, as a filling or sandwich spread. Fried, it makes a great main dish or burger substitute.

2 $1/2$ cups soybeans, soaked in 2 $1/2$ cups water overnight

1 cup cornmeal

1 $1/2$ cups nutritional yeast

1 tablespoon dried parsley

3 tablespoons dried sage

1 tablespoon fennel seed

3 tablespoons dried thyme

1 tablespoon salt

1 tablespoon ground allspice

1 tablespoon molasses

2 tablespoons honey

3 tablespoons yellow, spicy brown or partially ground prepared mustard

2 teaspoons ground pepper

$1/3$ cup tamari sauce

$1/4$ cup canola oil

4 cups water

2 teaspoons hickory flavor (optional)

1. Drain soybeans, reserving liquid. Puree in a blender or food processor with $1/4$ of reserved liquid. Slowly add more liquid as needed for desired consistency.

2. Mix soybean puree and all remaining ingredients together.

3. Fill greased cans or greased wide-mouth straight-sided canning jars, three-fourths full. Cover with aluminum foil and hold it in place with rubber bands.

4. Place jars or cans on a trivet waist-deep in water in a covered pot and steam for

1 $^{1}/_{2}$ hours (a little longer if using large cans, or 30 minutes in a pressure cooker). Let cool, slice, and fry (or use in recipes).

Serves 8

Baked Tofu

A high-protein, low-fat dish.

> 2 pounds firm tofu, drained
> 1 tablespoon minced fresh ginger
> 3 tablespoons tamari sauce
> Goma-shio for sprinkling

1. Put tofu on a cutting board that is slightly tilted to allow water to drain away. Put a plate on top to press out water. Let drain for 1 hour.

2. Slice tofu $^{1}/_{4}$-inch thick. Mix ginger and tamari sauce.

3. Dip each tofu slice in tamari mixture and place on a baking sheet.

4. Bake in a preheated 350°F oven for 20 to 45 minutes. The longer you bake it, the chewier it becomes. If you let it bake too long, you get tofu jerky.

5. Sprinkle with goma-shio to serve.

Tofu Telephones

The children named these one night while playing with their dinners. They were pretending that they were telephone receivers. Whenever I put them in their lunch boxes, they used to promise to give me a call at noon.

12 ounces firm tofu, well drained
1 cup cooked brown rice
1 tablespoon tahini
1 teaspoon soy sauce
$1/4$ teaspoon Asian sesame oil
$1/2$ teaspoon salt
$1/2$ cup fresh bread crumbs or ground nuts for coating

1. In a bowl, mix all ingredients except bread crumbs or nuts together.

2. Shape into crescents and roll in bread crumbs or nuts. Bake in a preheated 350°F oven for 20 minutes. Good with a dipping sauce or gravy.

Serves 6

Chestnut Chapeaux

These are delicious cold.

I tablespoon butter

I tablespoon canola oil

I cup chopped celery

I cup chopped cabbage

I cup fresh bread crumbs, plus more if needed

I tablespoon nutritional yeast

$1/_4$ teaspoon each dried parsley, sage, rosemary, thyme, marjoram, and
    ground ginger

Pinch of pepper

3 cups cooked rice

$1/_4$ cup chopped fresh parsley

4 tablespoons tahini

Salt to taste

2 cups chopped chestnuts

1. In a saucepan, melt butter with oil over medium heat. Sauté celery and cabbage until soft, about 5 minutes. Stir in I cup bread crumbs and cook for 5 minutes.

2. Remove from heat and stir in all remaining ingredients.

3. Oil hands and shape mixture into 16 flat-bottomed balls. Add more bread crumbs as needed to give the desired consistency for shaping.

4. Bake in a preheated 300°F oven for 30 minutes.

Makes 16 balls; serves 8

Rice Nuggets Monadnock

These nuggets climbed Mt. Monadnock in New Hampshire (the second most climbed mountain in the world). Since it is nearby, we go up about two times a year.

2 cups finely chopped kale
1 cup fresh whole-wheat bread crumbs
2 cups cooked brown rice
$1/2$ cup pureed kidney beans
1 cup mashed cooked pumpkin or squash
$1/2$ cup walnut meal (walnuts ground in a blender)

1. Lightly steam the kale over boiling water in a covered pot until wilted, about 5 minutes.

2. Add half of the bread crumbs and all remaining ingredients.

3. Roll into 1-inch balls and roll in bread crumbs.

4. Place on an oiled baking sheet and bake in a preheated 350°F oven for 30 minutes, or until golden brown.

Serves 6

Ginger-Tofu Steamed Buns

These are good with Spicy Tofu Mayonnaise (page 164).

Filling
1 pound firm tofu, mashed
1 tablespoon grated fresh ginger
1 tablespoon tamari sauce
2 tablespoons sesame seeds
Pinch of salt
1 teaspoon canola oil

Dough wrapper
1 cup warm (105° to 115°F) water
1 teaspoon active dried yeast
1 teaspoon honey
1 tablespoon canola oil
$1/2$ teaspoon salt
2 $1/4$ cups white unbleached flour

1. Mix filling ingredients and set aside.

2. In a bowl, mix warm water, yeast, and honey. Let sit for 5 minutes, or until foamy.

3. Stir in oil and salt. Stir in flour $1/2$ cup at a time. Kneed 15 minutes. Form into a ball. Place in an oiled bowl. Let rise in a warm place for 45 minutes.

4. Punch down. Divide into 12 pieces. Form each piece of dough into a ball. On a floured surface, roll each ball into a 3-inch round circle. Put about 2 tablespoons of filling in center of each round.

5. Gather up all edges of each round and pinch together to close. Set in a warm place, seam-side down, on a steaming rack for 15 minutes to rise.

6. Steam over boiling water in a covered pot for 15 minutes.

Variation: Combine 2 cups cooked adzuki beans and 2 cups pitted dates in a blender and puree. Use in place of filling in above recipe.

Makes 12 buns; serves 6

Rice Balls

I like these with spicy Tofu Mayonnaise (page 164) for a dipping sauce.

1 teaspoon tahini
1 tablespoon cornstarch
5 cups warm cooked rice
1 cup shredded cheese (optional)
$1/2$ cup mashed firm tofu
$1/4$ cup tomato sauce
$1/2$ teaspoon salt
$3/4$ cup cooked chickpeas or green peas
$2/3$ cup finely chopped almonds

1. Mix tahini and cornstarch into rice.

2. In a bowl, combine all other ingredients to make a stuffing.

3. Put about $1/3$ cup of the rice mixture in your cupped hand, leaving a little hollow in the center.

4. Put about 2 tablespoons stuffing in the hollow, sprinkle more rice mixture over the top, and pack. Resprinkle any areas where stuffing peeks through and pack well again.

5. Place on an oiled baking sheet. Bake in a preheated 350°F oven for 20 minutes, or until golden.

Makes about 12 balls; serves 6

Chili Fingers

$^1/_4$ cup olive oil
I cup chopped cabbage
$^1/_2$ green bell pepper, seeded, deribbed, and chopped
I cup tomato puree
I tablespoon chili powder
I cup chopped Soy Scrapple (page 132)
I pound bread dough

1. In a saucepan, heat oil over medium heat and sauté cabbage and green pepper for 5 to 8 minutes.

2. Add tomato puree, chili powder, and Soy Scrapple. Simmer for 10 minutes.

3. Divide bread dough into 18 pieces. Roll each piece into a strip 3-inches wide and $^1/_8$-inch thick.

4. Spread chili mixture about $^1/_4$-inch thick over each rectangle.

5. Starting with a long side, roll up into long ropes and place on an oiled baking sheet.

6. Place in a cold oven. Set temperature to 350°F and bake for 35 minutes, or until golden.

Variation: If you haven't any Soy Scrapple in the freezer, use 1 cup steamed soy grits or steamed texturized vegetable protein (TVP), but increase the chili powder another 2 teaspoons and simmer for about 15 minutes.

Makes about 18 fingers; serves 5

Spring Rolls

Spiced dried tofu is sometimes available in Asian food stores. I usually don't have it, so I simmer firm tofu, finely diced, in tamari and ginger until very firm, 10 to 15 minutes.

2 cups bean sprouts, chopped
3 cups shredded cabbage
2 cups shredded spinach
1 cup shredded carrots or other vegetables (optional)
$3/4$ cup spiced tofu, finely diced
3 cups cooked bean thread noodles (cellophane noodles), chopped
12 spring roll wrappers (some wrappers are made with eggs, others not)
Canola oil

1. In a bowl, combine all vegetables, tofu, and noodles. In a saucepan, cook mixture in a little water until vegetables are just wilted. Drain.

2. Place about 3 tablespoons of filling in center of a wrapper. Fold bottom corner up over filling and tuck in sides, then roll up. When you reach last corner, dip your fingers in water and rub flap to seal it (rubbing a bit of cornstarch on corner will help). Repeat to fill remaining wrappers.

3. In a skillet, heat 1-inch deep oil over medium heat. Place rolls, seam-side down, in skillet. Cook on both sides until golden.

4. Using tongs, transfer to paper towels to drain. Send along a cup of Sweet & Sour Sauce (page 169) for dipping.

Variation: For a lowfat variation, I often make these with 8-inch round rice papers that have been soaked for a few minutes and then drained. Fold in same manner.

Makes 12 rolls; serves 12

Madhuri's Ricotta Quiche

This was the favorite food of a sweet young girl I knew in Vermont. She's a young woman now. I wonder if she eats her vegetables yet?

   2 pounds ricotta cheese
   $1/2$ cup grated Parmesan cheese
   9-inch unbaked pie crust

1. In a bowl, mix cheeses together.

2. Spread into pie crust and bake in a preheated 350°F oven for 30 minutes.

   Variation: Stir in 1 cup chopped steamed spinach

Makes one 9-inch quiche; serves 6

Soy Soufflé

This tastes good with Spicy Tofu Mayonnaise (page 164), mustard, and pickles.

2 cups chopped tomatoes
$1/2$ cup water
$1/4$ teaspoon dried parsley
$1/4$ teaspoon dried basil
$1/4$ teaspoon hing (asafetida)
$1/4$ cup grated Parmesan cheese
$1/4$ cup peanut butter
$1/4$ teaspoon salt
1 cup soy flour
Few drops Asian sesame oil

1. Combine tomatoes, water, herbs, Parmesan cheese, peanut butter, and salt in a blender or food processor and process until smooth.

2. With motor running, gradually add soy flour, then oil.

3. Pour into 1-inch deep quart-sized baking dish and bake in a preheated 450°F for 15 minutes.

4. Lower heat to 250°F and bake another 45 minutes. Cover and let cool. Slice cold.

Serves 4

Yeasty Vegetarian Omelettes

Package a bit of chutney to eat along with these.

I cup nutritional yeast

I cup unbleached white bread flour

I teaspoon curry powder

$^1/_2$ teaspoon salt

8 ounces firm or extra-firm tofu

I $^1/_2$ cups water

$^1/_4$ cup chopped cabbage

I tablespoon sunflower seeds

$^1/_4$ cup chopped celery

$^1/_4$ cup shredded Cheddar cheese

$^1/_4$ cup grated carrot

1. In a bowl, mix yeast, flour, curry powder, and salt together.

2. Process tofu and water in a blender until smooth. Add to dry ingredients.

3. Fold in all remaining ingredients until blended.

4. Heat an oiled skillet over medium heat. Pour out 3-inch rounds and cook until golden on both sides.

Serves 4

Vermont Nut Loaf

This delicious loaf has a lot of protein. I'm not quite sure of its origins; I used to call my friend Cirasmita in Vermont whenever I needed the recipe, just as she called me every summer to get the recipe for dill pickles. I've finally managed to hang on to it.

2 tablespoons butter

1 cup chopped celery

1 cup chopped cabbage

$1/2$ cup sesame seed meal (grind seeds in blender or food processor)

$1/2$ cup sunflower seed meal (grind seeds in blender or food processor)

1 pound cottage cheese, or 2 cups mashed extra-firm tofu

3 tablespoons powdered soy milk

$1/2$ cup cooked brown rice

$1/2$ teaspoon each dried parsley and thyme

$1/2$ cup rolled oats or fresh bread crumbs

1 cup chopped toasted almonds

1 cup chopped pecans or walnuts

1 cup chopped toasted cashews

$1/4$ to $1/2$ cup water

1. Melt butter in a saucepan over medium heat. Sauté vegetables for 5 minutes.

2. Add all remaining ingredients and mix.

3. Pack into an oiled 5- x 9-inch or 4- x 8-inch loaf pan. Bake in a preheated 375°F oven for 1 hour and 15 minutes, or until firm.

Makes 1 loaf; serves 6

Sombreros

Send along a small container of yogurt for topping.

3 tablespoons canola oil
2 cups shredded cabbage
1 green bell pepper, chopped
1 cup chopped celery
$1/4$ teaspoon dried thyme
$1/4$ teaspoon cayenne pepper
$1/4$ teaspoon hing (asafetida)
1 teaspoon salt
3 cups cooked pinto beans
2 cups corn kernels
$1/2$ cup tomato puree
2 teaspoons ground cumin

Spiced Cornmeal Crust
3 cups water
1 $3/4$ cups cornmeal
$1/2$ teaspoon ground cumin
Pinch of salt
Dash of cayenne pepper
1 cup finely chopped olives
$1/2$ cup shredded Monterey Jack cheese for garnish

1. In a saucepan, heat oil over medium heat and sauté cabbage, bell pepper, and celery until cabbage is soft, about 5 minutes.

2. Add thyme, cayenne, hing, salt, beans, corn, tomato puree, and cumin. Simmer until it thickens, about 15 minutes. Set aside.

3. To make spiced cornmeal crust, in a saucepan stir all ingredients except olives together. Cook until thick as pudding, about 30 minutes, stirring constantly. Add olives.

4. Spread half of cornmeal mixture (while still warm) in a greased shallow baking dish. Spread bean mixture over. Sprinkle with cheese. Spread on remaining cornmeal mix.

5. Bake in a preheated 350°F oven for about 30 minutes, or until golden brown. Let cool for 15 minutes. Cut into 6 squares.

Serves 6

Gluten

Gluten is the protein part of the wheat. It is starchless and makes a great meat substitute, usually sold as seitan. The longer you knead and simmer gluten, the tougher it will be. You can achieve a whole range of textures, from soft dumpling to meatlike chewiness.

> 1 cup unbleached gluten flour
> 1 cup water
> Brown Broth (page 70) for Brown Gluten, or Yellow Broth (page 69) for
> Yellow Gluten

Quick Method
1. In a bowl, stir together gluten flour and water, adding more water if necessary to achieve a thick dough.

2. Knead dough for 10 minutes to develop elasticity in gluten and squeeze out excess water.

3. Bring broth to a boil. Break gluten into small pieces about 1 inch in diameter and drop into boiling broth.

4. Simmer for at least 30 minutes. Gluten gets firmer the longer it is cooked.

Variation: If you cannot get gluten flour, follow these steps: Mix together and knead 6 cups bread flour (which happens to be high in gluten) and 1 $^1/_2$ cups water for about 20 minutes. Submerge the dough in a bowl of cold water for 1 hour. Start kneading dough underwater (gently at first). The water will turn white as starch is released into it. Pour off this water and continue kneading under fresh water. Repeat until water clears. Follow directions, starting with number 3, above.

Brown Gluten: Simmer gluten in Brown Broth (page 70).
Yellow Gluten: Simmer gluten in Yellow Broth (page 69).

Serves 6

Savory Vegetable Cake

When the cake is cold, thermos-held hot Marsha's Vegetable Broth Gravy (page 73) is nice poured over it.

> 3 tablespoons butter
> $^1/_2$ cup grated carrot
> 1 cup corn kernels
> $^1/_2$ cup chopped broccoli
> $^1/_2$ cup cooked kidney beans
> $^1/_2$ cup chopped pitted black olives
> 1 $^1/_2$ teaspoons baking powder
> $^3/_4$ cup milk, soy milk, or nut milk
> $^1/_4$ cup plain yogurt
> 2 tablespoons tahini
> 1 teaspoon chopped fresh parsley
> Pinch of pepper

1 tablespoon sunflower seeds
$^1/_2$ cup grated Parmesan cheese
1 $^1/_2$ cups whole-wheat flour
$^1/_4$ cup nutritional yeast
1 teaspoon salt

1. Melt butter in an ovenproof skillet over medium heat and sauté vegetables until they turn bright. Add beans and olives and set aside.

2. In a bowl, mix all remaining ingredients until smooth.

3. Pour batter over vegetables in skillet. Bake in a preheated 300°F oven for 45 minutes.

4. Flip cake over onto a plate and cut into 6 wedges. Eat hot or cold.

Makes 1 cake; serves 6

Honey-Fried Tofu

1 pound firm tofu, drained
2 tablespoons honey
1 tablespoon butter
Salt to taste

1. Cut tofu into $^1/_2$-inch cubes.

2. In a heavy skillet, melt butter over medium-high heat. Add honey and stir in tofu.

3. Fry until golden on both sides. Add salt to taste.

Serves 4

Vegetarian Sushi (Nori Rolls)

Experiment with these. I have used sweet pickles in them and grated ginger into horseradish for sauce. Sometimes, I add raisins, avocado, or chestnuts.

1 pound Baked Tofu (page 133)
1 cucumber, peeled
1 carrot, peeled
6 sheets nori seaweed
3 cups cooked brown rice
1 umoboshi plum, pureed to a paste
2 tablespoons pickled ginger
1 tablespoon Spicy Tofu Mayonnaise (page 164), wasabi powder plus water
    as needed, or prepared horseradish

1. Slice tofu, cucumber, and carrot into matchsticks.

2. Place a sheet of nori on a cutting board and spread about $1/_2$ cup brown rice on nori sheet, leaving a $1/_2$-inch margin on far edge.

3. Place a little bundle of matchsticks in center and sprinkle lightly with bits of umoboshi paste.

4. Roll up going towards the seaweed margin. Wet margin and seal. Wrap in waxed paper and twist ends. Repeat for each roll.

5. To eat, open one end and peel waxed paper down as you eat. Or, slice into $3/_4$-inch tall rounds and top each with a bit of pickled ginger and wasabi paste. Eat with Spicy Tofu Mayonnaise (page 164) or horseradish.

Makes 6 rolls; serves 6

Basic Burgers

These burgers can be seasoned as you like. The amount of nuts and seeds can be increased or left out. You can use any beans, or leftover bean soup, and any grains, including leftover cooked breakfast cereal. You can practically empty the refrigerator, just as with minestrone soup. I have a son who won't eat his crusts, so I indulge him. I cut them off his sandwiches, and I save them for burgers.

2 cups cooked beans, mashed
$1/2$ cup stock or water (if the beans are a bit dry)
1 cup cooked rice, millet, bulgur, and so on
1 cup toasted chopped nuts or seeds
2 tablespoons nutritional yeast
$1/4$ cup tamari sauce
$1/4$ teaspoon dried oregano
$1/4$ teaspoon dried thyme
Salt and pepper to taste
$1/2$ cup shredded carrots or finely chopped cooked vegetables
2 cups rolled oats or fresh bread crumbs, use more as needed
Canola oil (optional)

1. In a bowl, combine all ingredients except oats or bread crumbs and optional oil.

2. Add oats or bread crumbs as needed to stiffen mixture.

3. Form into 8 patties. Fry in oil over medium heat in a skillet, or bake in a preheated 350°F oven for 30 minutes.

Serves 8

Tofu Quiche

Great hot or cold.

   2 tablespoons butter
   3 tablespoons whole-wheat flour
   $1/4$ cup milk
   $1/4$ teaspoon paprika
   $1/2$ teaspoon salt
   1 $1/2$ cup shredded sharp Cheddar cheese
   1 $1/2$ pounds extra-firm or firm tofu, mashed
   1 pound fresh spinach, stemmed, chopped, and steamed until wilted, or one
      10-ounce package frozen spinach, thawed
   9-inch pie crust, unbaked

1. Melt butter in a saucepan over medium-low heat.

2. Add flour and stir for 3 minutes. Gradually whisk in milk. Add paprika and salt. Cook, stirring, until thickened.

3. Stir in cheese, tofu, and spinach until blended.

4. Fill pie crust and bake in a preheated 350°F oven for 30 minutes.

Makes one 9-inch quiche; serves 6

Falafels

These are traditionally stuffed in pita bread, but my kids like me to send along a cocktail sword so that they can spear them and dip them in Cranberry Ketchup (page 159) or Peach Chutney (page 160).

> 2 tablespoons olive oil
> $1/2$ cup finely chopped green bell pepper
> 1 cup finely chopped cabbage
> 2 cups Soy Puree (page 153)
> 1 tablespoon dried parsley
> 2 tablespoons tahini
> 1 teaspoon ground cumin
> $1/4$ teaspoon ground pepper
> 1 to 1 $1/2$ cups fresh bread crumbs

1. In a skillet, heat oil over medium heat and sauté green pepper and cabbage for 5 minutes.

2. In a bowl, combine cooked vegetables with all remaining ingredients, using enough bread crumbs to hold it together.

3. Roll into 18 balls the size of large marbles. Place on an oiled baking sheet. Flatten each ball slightly. Bake for about 15 minutes in a preheated 300°F oven.

Makes 18 falafels; serves 6

Soy Puree

1 $^1/_2$ cups chickpeas
4 cups water

1. Soak chickpeas overnight. Drain.

2. In a saucepan, simmer chickpeas in 4 cups water for about 1 hour, or until soft enough to squish between your thumb and forefinger. Drain, reserving 2 cups water.

3. In a blender, puree chickpeas, adding reserved water as needed for desired consistency.

   Note: If using canned chickpeas, puree in blender adding canning liquid as needed for desired consistency.

Simple Vegetable Pizzas

1 recipe bread dough
2 green bell peppers, seeded, deribbed, and chopped
1 small can black olives, drained and sliced
2 cups sliced or diced tomatoes (use halved cherry tomatoes, sliced large tomatoes, or even drained canned diced tomatoes)
2 cups shredded Cheddar cheese

1. Divide bread dough into 6 pieces.

2. Roll each out on a floured board into $^1/_4$-inch-thick rounds.

3. Place rounds on a baking sheet dusted with cornmeal. Sprinkle vegetables over rounds.

4. Top with cheese.

5. Let rise for 25 minutes in a warm place.

6. Bake in a preheated 400°F oven for 20 to 25 minutes, or until cheese is melted and golden colored.

Makes 6 pizzas; serves 6

Spinach Pizzas

I recipe bread dough
I 10-ounce package frozen spinach, or 2 cups fresh spinach, stemmed and
    steamed until wilted
I small can black olives, drained and sliced
6 ounces feta cheese
Juice of I lemon
4 tablespoons olive oil
Pepper to taste

1. Divide dough into 6 pieces. Form into balls. Roll each ball out on a floured board into $^1/_4$-inch-thick rounds.

2. Place rounds on a baking sheet sprinkled with cornmeal. Spread spinach over rounds. Sprinkle with olives and feta cheese. Drizzle lemon juice and olive oil over all. Add pepper.

3. Let rise for 20 minutes. Bake in a preheated 400°F oven for 20 to 25 minutes, or until crust is golden brown on edges.

Makes 6 pizzas; serves 6

CHAPTER 6

Condiments, Sauces, & Snacks

Chapter Contents

CHAPTER 6

Condiments, Sauces & Snacks

Whenever I think of packing condiments and dips for lunch, I think of the little badger named Francis in Russel Hoban's book *Bread and Jam for Francis*. She brings her lunch to school (after being cured of a desire for meals of only bread and jam) and lays a paper doily on her desk, sets a tiny vase of violets in the middle of it, and arranges around it her lunch of:

> a thermos bottle with cream of tomato soup, a lobster salad sandwich on thin slices of white bread, celery, carrot sticks, and black olives, and a little cardboard shaker of salt for the celery. And two plums and a tiny basket of cherries. And vanilla pudding with chocolate sprinkles and a spoon to eat it with.

My family loves dipping, dunking, sprinkling, pouring, and generally playing with their food, so these recipes are well used.

Quick Ketchup

8 cups tomato puree

6 ounces tomato paste

2 teaspoons salt

3 green bell peppers, seeded, deribbed, and chopped

1 tablespoon celery seed

1 $1/2$ teaspoons ground allspice

1 $1/2$ bay leaves

$3/4$ cup honey

$1/4$ cup molasses

1 $1/2$ cups cider vinegar

1. Combine all ingredients in a pot. Simmer for about 20 minutes, or until thickened.

2. Remove bay leaf. Puree in batches in a blender.

3. Store in a jar in the refrigerator for up to 2 weeks, or process $1/2$-pint jars in a boiling-water bath for 20 minutes to can.

Makes about 8 cups

Cranberry Ketchup

This is good with curried foods and nut loaves.

    I pound fresh or frozen cranberries
    I cup water
    $1/2$ cup molasses
    $1/2$ cup honey
    $1/2$ cup cider vinegar
    $1/4$ teaspoon ground allspice
    $1/4$ teaspoon ground cloves
    I teaspoon salt

1. In a saucepan, simmer cranberries in water until they pop and soften, about 15 minutes.

2. Puree in blender or food processor until smooth. Return to pan and stir in remaining ingredients. Simmer for 20 minutes. Let cool. Freeze or store in refrigerator for up to 3 weeks.

Makes about 3 cups

Peach Chutney

5 peaches, peeled, pitted, and chopped

6 ripe tomatoes, peeled and chopped

5 green apples, peeled, cored, and chopped

1 green bell pepper, seeded, deribbed, and chopped

$1/_2$ cup cider vinegar

1 teaspoon ground ginger

1 teaspoon mustard seeds

1 teaspoon salt

$3/_4$ cup honey

1. Combine all ingredients except honey in a saucepan. Simmer for 20 minutes.

2. Stir in honey and simmer until thickened, about 15 minutes.

3. Pour into hot sterilized half-pint jars and seal. Process in a hot-water bath for 10 minutes. Once opened, keeps in the refrigerator for up to 1 week.

D.V.'s Green Tomato Relish

My friend D.V.'s family eats a lot of condiments with their meals, hence the amounts here. It is a good way to use up green tomatoes. I make this every other year, give a few jars away, and we have enough for 2 years.

    1 gallon apples, cored, peeled, and quartered
    1 gallon green tomatoes, quartered
    4 bell peppers, seeded, and deribbed
    1 bunch celery
    4 cups cider vinegar
    2 cups honey
    1 teaspoon ground cloves
    1 teaspoon ground allspice
    1 teaspoon salt
    1 teaspoon mustard seeds

1. Finely chop apples and vegetables. Drain.

2. In a large pot, mix all ingredients together and simmer until tender, about 10 minutes. Process in a hot-water bath for 10 minutes. Opened jars can be refrigerated for up to 1 month.

3. Pour into hot sterilized pint jars and seal.

Makes about 16 pints

D.V.'s Mincemeat

12 green tomatoes, finely chopped

4 cups honey

2 cups raisins

5 cooking apples, cored, peeled, and finely chopped

1 tablespoon salt

1 tablespoon ground cinnamon

1 tablespoon ground allspice

1 tablespoon ground cloves

1. Drain tomatoes and put in a large pot. Stir in 1 cup of the honey.

2. Simmer mixture for 10 minutes, or until apples are tender.

3. Add remaining honey and all remaining ingredients. Simmer for 45 minutes.

4. Pour into hot sterilized pint jars, and seal. Process in a hot-water bath for 10 minutes. Opened jars can be refrigerated for 1 to 2 weeks.

Makes about 10 pints

Nut Milk

1 cup raw nuts, such as almonds, cashews, or peanuts

4 cups boiling water

Salt to taste

Honey to taste

In batches, combine nuts and water in a blender and puree. Stir in salt and honey.

Makes 4 cups

Nut Milk Mayonnaise

This can be used in recipes calling for mayonnaise or Tofu Mayonnaise. Use sparingly.

3 tablespoons honey
$1/2$ teaspoon sea salt or to taste
$1/2$ teaspoon dill seed
$1/2$ teaspoon paprika
1 tablespoon yellow or light brown prepared mustard
1 cup Nut Milk (page 162)
1 $1/2$ cups canola oil
$1/4$ cup fresh lemon juice or cider vinegar

1. Process all ingredients except oil and lemon juice or vinegar in a blender.

2. With motor running, drizzle in the oil until thickened.

3. Stir in lemon juice or vinegar. Store in refrigerator for up to 2 weeks.

Makes about 3 cups

Tofu Mayonnaise

The oil can be left out of this recipe to make it low in fat. I often make sandwiches of whole-grain bread, sliced vegetables, and Tofu Mayonnaise, for a high-protein lunch.

1 $1/2$ pounds firm tofu
2 tablespoons tahini
1 teaspoon dill seed
$1/4$ cup cider vinegar
2 tablespoons prepared yellow mustard
$1/2$ teaspoon ground turmeric (optional)
$1/4$ cup honey
$1/3$ cup canola oil (optional)
Salt to taste

1. Combine all ingredients in blender in batches and puree. Add milk if needed to desired consistency.

2. Adjust seasoning to suit your taste.

Variation: Spicy Tofu Mayonnaise: Add 2 tablespoons wasabi powder, $1/2$ teaspoon chili oil, and 2 teaspoons tamari sauce to Tofu Mayonnaise.

Makes 2 $1/2$ cups

Nut Cream

Tastes nice on puddings, fruit gels, or cold baked apples.

I cup raw cashews or almonds
$^1/_4$ cup honey
2 cups water
Dash of vanilla extract
Pinch of salt

Blend all ingredients together in a blender. Store in a covered container in the refrigerator for I to 2 days.

Makes 2 $^1/_2$ cups

Eggplant Aside

When our older child Amber was little. She couldn't bear to have different items touching each other, so everything had to be put on the side. This got shortened to aside and all condiments became asides.

I globe eggplant, peeled and chopped
$^1/_4$ cup olive oil
2 teaspoons sesame seeds
I cup chopped cabbage
I stalk celery, chopped
4 tomatoes, chopped
2 teaspoons honey
$^1/_4$ cup tarragon vinegar or other herbed vinegar
$^1/_4$ cup pickled nasturtium buds
Salt and pepper to taste

1. Lightly steam eggplant over boiling water in a covered pot for 10 to 15 minutes.

2. Combine oil and sesame seeds in skillet over medium heat. Add eggplant, cabbage, and celery and sauté for 10 minutes.

3. Add tomatoes, honey, vinegar, nasturtium buds, salt, and pepper. Simmer for about 20 minutes. Store in refrigerator for up to 2 weeks.

Makes 4 to 5 cups

Picada

Try this wrapped in pita pockets or Yeasty Crepes (page 12); do this on site, or it will be soggy.

Paste
$1/4$ teaspoon hing (asafetida)
$1/4$ teaspoon powdered saffron
$1/4$ teaspoon salt
$1/4$ teaspoon ground cinnamon
1 teaspoon chopped fresh parsley
$1/2$ cup toasted almonds
$1/2$ cup toasted hazelnuts
$1/2$ cup white wine

1 cup firm tofu, drained and cubed
1 cup chopped tomatoes
1 cup chopped eggplant
1 cup chopped green bell pepper
$1/2$ cup black olives, chopped

1. Grind all paste ingredients together in a blender or food processor.

2. In a saucepan, combine paste and vegetables.

3. Simmer until tender, about 20 minutes. Let cool.

4. Add olives.

Lemon-Honey Jelly

This is good with spicy or fried foods. I also give the kids a teaspoonful if they are coughing at night.

>   5 cups honey
>   1 $1/2$ cups water
>   6 ounces liquid pectin
> $1/3$ cup fresh lemon juice

1. In a saucepan, boil the honey and water.

2. Add pectin and boil 2 minutes more.

3. Remove from heat and stir in lemon juice.

4. Pour into hot sterilized half-pint jars and seal. Process in a hot-water bath for 10 minutes.

Makes about 7 half-pints

Herbed Yogurt Cheese

2 cups yogurt cheese
$1/4$ cup dried vegetable flakes
Pinch of garlic
Pinch of salt
Dash of tamari
Quick grating of black pepper

In a bowl, stir all together, and let meld overnight. The vegetable flakes will plump up, and the cheese will dry a little. Store covered in refrigerator for up to a week.

Pesto Sentio

This was named by my last editor. She named it Sentio after the world sentient. Sentient is a yogic category of foods that are good for meditation. Because this has no garlic, it falls into that category.

This is a good basic pesto. It has a highly concentrated taste. As it is high in fat, use sparingly or stretch it with extenders as in Pestofu (page 45). Other spices or cheeses can be added.

4 cups fresh basil
$1/2$ cup cashews, or $1/4$ cup almond butter
$1/2$ cup olive oil
Salt to taste

1. Combine all ingredients in a blender and process until smooth.

2. Keep in a covered container in the refrigerator for up to 2 weeks, or freeze in small jars for up to 1 year (the olive oil helps with preservation).

Makes about 1 $1/2$ cups

Sweet & Sour Sauce

Good with Spring Rolls (page 140) and spicy foods.

> 6 cups chopped fruit (peaches, plums, pineapples)
> 1 $^1/_2$ cups water
> 1 tablespoon tamari sauce
> $^1/_2$ cup honey
> $^1/_2$ teaspoon salt
> 1 tablespoon arrowroot, cornstarch, or tapioca flour
> $^1/_3$ cup cider vinegar

1. Combine fruit and water in a saucepan and simmer until tender, about 10 to 15 minutes.

2. Mash gently and stir in all remaining ingredients. Simmer for 5 minutes. Keeps in a covered container in the refrigerator for up to 2 weeks.

Makes about 6 cups

Delectable Yam Sauce

Try this poured on cold steamed broccoli and cauliflower, or mix it with leftover stir-fried vegetables and pack it hot into a thermos. Very high in A and B vitamins and protein.

$^1/_2$ cup peanut butter

1 to 3 cups water

2 cups mashed cooked yams or sweet potatoes

$^3/_4$ cup nutritional yeast

2 tablespoons tamari sauce

$^1/_2$ teaspoon salt

1 teaspoon paprika

1 teaspoon ground turmeric

1 $^1/_2$ teaspoons ground cumin

1. In a saucepan, stir peanut butter and 1 cup of the water together.

2. Add all remaining ingredients plus water to desired thickness. Simmer for 10 minutes. Store in refrigerator for up to 1 week.

Makes about 4 $^1/_2$ cups

Sunflower Seed Sauce

This sauce tastes good on steamed green beans or steamed greens.

    1 cup sunflower seeds
    $1/3$ cup water
    2 tablespoons fresh lemon juice
    Salt to taste

Process all ingredients together in a blender.

Makes about $1/2$ cup

Rhubarb Sauce

This makes a good dipping sauce for Falafels (page 152) or Garbanzo Chips (page 16).

    2 cups rhubarb cut in 1-inch chunks
    $1/2$ cup water
    $1/2$ cup honey
    1 teaspoon Dijon mustard
    Juice of $1/2$ lemon
    $1/4$ teaspoon salt
    Pinch of wasabi powder

1. In a covered pot, simmer rhubarb for about 15 minutes, or until very tender and mushy.

2. In a bowl, combine all ingredients in a blender.

3. Store in a covered jar in the refrigerator for up to 2 weeks, or freeze in $^1/_2$-pint jars for up to 6 months.

Makes about 2 cups

Tofu Tartar Sauce

1 cup Tofu Mayonnaise (page 164)
1 cup D.V.'s Green Tomato Relish (page 161)
1 tablespoon pickled nasturtium buds or capers (optional)

Stir all ingredients together until blended. Keeps in a covered container in the refrigerator for up to 2 weeks.

Makes 2 cups

Barbecue Sauce

4 tablespoons canola oil
1 cup chopped cabbage
$^1/_2$ teaspoon hing (asafetida)
2 cups tomato puree
$^1/_2$ cup honey
$^1/_2$ cup molasses
1 tablespoon salt
1 tablespoon dry mustard
Pinch of cayenne pepper
$^1/_2$ teaspoon ground allspice

$^1/_2$ cup cider vinegar

$^1/_8$ cup tamari sauce

1. Heat oil in a saucepan over medium heat and sauté cabbage until translucent.

2. Add all ingredients except vinegar and tamari. Reduce heat and simmer for 45 minutes.

3. Add vinegar and tamari. Simmer for 10 minutes. Freeze or store in refrigerator for up to 3 weeks.

Makes 4 cups

Spanish Hazelnut Sauce

This sauce is also high in fat. Not as much as straight butter, oil, or sour cream, but still it should be used sparingly like salad dressing is. I like it on mild vegetables such as summer squash or zucchini.

2 tablespoons chopped fresh basil

$^1/_4$ teaspoon hing (asafetida)

$^1/_2$ cup toasted hazelnuts

$^1/_2$ cup toasted almonds

1 cup tomato puree

$^1/_2$ cup olive oil

1 tablespoon cider vinegar

1 tablespoon molasses

1. Puree all ingredients together in a blender.

2. Pour into a saucepan and simmer for 20 minutes.

3. Keeps in a covered jar in the refrigerator for up to 2 weeks, or freeze in small jars for up to 6 months.

Makes about 2 cups

Snacks

Crunchings & Munchings

This mix was named for a beloved book friend, Gurgi. He's always hungry and begs for "crunchings and munchings." It is gorp (the stuff you eat on hiking trips), lightened with puffed cereal. Mix in proportions suitable to your taste.

$1/2$ cup raisins
$1/2$ cup chopped dried apples
$1/2$ cup sunflower seeds
$1/2$ cup chopped almonds
$1/2$ cup chocolate or carob chips
1 cup puffed rice
1 cup puffed wheat

In a bowl, combine all ingredients and stir to mix. Store in an airtight container in the refrigerator for up to 2 weeks.

Makes 4 $1/2$ cups

Soy Nuts or Chickpea Nuts

1 cup dried soybeans or chickpeas, rinsed
3 cups water
1 teaspoon salt

1. Wash soybeans.

2. Soak beans in salted water overnight. Drain.

3. Roast beans on an unoiled baking sheet, one layer deep, in a preheated 250°F oven for about 2 hours, stirring occasionally.

Makes 2 cups

Popcorn

Popcorn can be flavored to make different snacks. Try one of the following:

Grated Parmesan cheese
Chili powder to taste
Curry powder to taste
Nutritional yeast (my kids' favorite) to taste

After popcorn is popped, mist with a little oil and sprinkle on a dry topping.

Toasted Nuts & Seeds

Nuts and seeds can be toasted on a dry cast-iron skillet, stirring often, or toasted in a preheated 300°F oven for 30 minutes, stirring less often. Let cool before storing in airtight jars. If you like slightly salty nuts, try soaking them overnight in salted water first. Nuts are more nutritious if semisprouted and dried. Soak raw nuts overnight in salt water, drain, and bake in an oven or dehydrator at 150°F for about 18 hours. When cool, store in airtight jars.

Every diet needs a little fat to be healthy. Oils are sometimes chemically extracted or exposed to extreme heat which alters their digestibility. By using a light mist of raw organic oil or tiny portions of nuts, seeds, olives, or avocados, we can get a healthy form and amount of fat in our diets.

Vegetable & Fruit Snacks

Vegetable Slices

Fresh vegetables are wonderful for scooping up dips. Try slicing them into these different shapes to better enjoy their wonderful textures and flavors: matchsticks, lengthwise slices, ovals made by slicing carrots, zucchini, or cucumbers diagonally.

Green beans or sugar snap peas need no cutting. Turnips, rutabagas, and kohlrabi are delicious sliced thin as chips. If you are preparing broccoli for supper, save the stalks to cut into lengthwise slices for lunch the following day.

Dried Vegetables & Fruits

Slice carrots, zucchini, or bananas thinly and place on a mesh tray in a dehydrator until crunchy, or dry on a baking sheet in a 150°F oven for 6 to 8 hours, turning when top is crisp and bottom of each chip is only leathery. This will crisp both sides. Use vegetable chips with dip in place of potato chips. Cut corn can also be dehydrated and turns out nice and crunchy.

Fruit Leathers

These are incredibly easy to make, especially with a dehydrator. They keep for months and nicely use up an overabundance of seasonal fruit.

To make leather, remove pit or seeds from fruit. Put fruit in a blender with enough water to blend. Pour the resulting puree on a plastic drying sheet and dehydrate on low until leathery. Dehydrators have some solid plastic drying sheets for runny foods.

If using a parked-car back window, oven, or other heat source, pour the puree on waxed paper on a baking sheet, expose to gentle heat and leave room for air circulation (crack open oven door or car window).

Leathers can be eaten plain or filled. Roll a piece around a cheese finger, or spread with cream cheese, roll up, and slice.

Jam

Jam can be made by dehydrating puree halfway to leather. It can be sweetened if desired. We make a brilliant scarlet strawberry jam this way.

Yogurt Chips

These can be made by dropping little bits of flavored yogurt on a plastic tray and dehydrating.

CHAPTER 7

Desserts

Chapter Contents

CHAPTER 7

Desserts

Great lunches can be centered around a dessert, for example, green salad with a squash pie, or clear vegetable soup and cheesecake. Many recipes we traditionally think of as dessert are high in protein and quite worthy on their own.

Tofu is a good egg substitute, and soy flour can replace some of the wheat-flour in a recipe, to boost the protein. Nuts and seeds can be ground and added to many recipes. Cream cheese, ricotta cheese, and pureed cottage cheese can be added to almost anything; apple pie tastes great with cheese in the filling or the crust; as the saying goes: "Apple pie without some cheese is like a kiss without the squeeze!"

Vegetables are also easy to add to desserts. Many of the milder-tasting vegetables, such as beets, corn, lima beans, and potatoes, can be used in the liquid portion of a recipe. Squash, yams, and carrots can be added to cakes and cookies to lend moistness and nutrition. When I bake something chocolate, I always add spinach powder or puree!

Egg Replacer for Baking

While not a dessert, the following recipe is useful in replacing eggs in many different kinds of desserts. It assists the rising and while it does not really act as a binder, it does give body to baked goods. I use it in cookies and cakes.

    8 ounces firm tofu
    2 tablespoons plain nonfat yogurt
    1 tablespoon cornstarch or arrowroot
    $1/2$ teaspoon baking soda

Process all ingredients together in a blender or food processor until smooth.

Replaces 2 eggs

Baked Sweet Potato

Bake a sweet potato for 45 minutes in a preheated 350°F oven. Send it in its skin. Peel and eat like a banana.

Medieval Honey Cake

$1/2$ cup apple butter

1 $1/2$ cups unbleached white flour (if using whole-wheat flour, reduce water
  to $3/4$ cups)

4 tablespoons butter, melted

1 teaspoon baking soda

$1/2$ teaspoon salt

$3/4$ cup honey

1 $1/2$ tablespoons cider vinegar

1 cup water

1 cup dried currants

1. In a bowl, whisk all ingredients except currants together. Stir in currants.

2. Pour into an ungreased 8-inch square baking pan. Bake in a preheated 350°F oven for about 30 minutes, or until it starts to pull away from edge of pan and a toothpick inserted in the middle comes out clean.

Makes one 8-inch square cake; serves 8

Lemon Cake: Omit currants. Add grated zest and juice of 1 lemon and 1 teaspoon lemon extract.

Spice Cake: Omit currants. Use molasses in place of honey and add 1 cup mashed squash or sweet potato. Reduce water to $1/2$ cup and add $1/2$ teaspoon each ground ginger, ground cloves, and ground cinnamon.

Chocolate or Carob Cake: Omit currants. Add 4 tablespoons carob powder or cocoa powder, $1/2$ cup more honey (to the cocoa), and 1 teaspoon vanilla extract.

Fruit Agar-Gel Mold

A vegetarian gelatin dessert.

> 2 cups chopped fruit, such as apples, oranges, bananas, grapes
> $1/2$ cup chopped nuts, coconut, or sunflower seeds
> 1 tablespoon granulated agar agar
> 3 cups fruit juice (try grapefruit or tangerine)

1. In a bowl, combine fruit and nuts, coconut, or sunflower seeds.

2. In a saucepan, mix agar agar with fruit juice and let sit for 5 minutes.

3. Bring to a boil and cook for 3 minutes, stirring.

4. Remove from heat. Let cool slightly. Fold in fruit mixture.

5. Pour into a 4- to 5-cup mold. Refrigerate for 1 to 2 hours, or until solid.

Makes 4 servings.

Kingsmont Peanut Butter Cake

> 8 ounces firm tofu
> 1 cup honey
> $1/2$ cup molasses
> 1 tablespoon vanilla extract
> 1 tablespoon cider vinegar
> 1 cup peanut butter
> 2 $1/2$ cups unbleached white, white-wheat, or whole-wheat pastry flour

1 teaspoon baking powder

1 teaspoon baking soda

1 $^1/_2$ teaspoons salt

1. Process tofu, honey, molasses, vanilla, vinegar, and peanut butter in a blender or food processor until smooth.

2. Pour into a bowl and stir in all remaining ingredients. Pour into a 9- x 12-inch dish. Bake in a preheated 350°F oven for 30 minutes, or until golden, pulling away from edge of pan, and a toothpick inserted in the center comes out clean.

Makes one 9- x 12-inch cake; serves 12

Halva

2 cups tahini at room temperature

$^3/_4$ cup honey

1 $^1/_2$ cups soy milk powder

$^1/_2$ cup carob powder

$^1/_2$ cup chopped pecans

1. In a bowl, stir together all ingredients except nuts.

2. Press about $^3/_4$-inch deep into a jelly roll pan.

3. Sprinkle with nuts and press into mixture. Refrigerate for about 2 hours. Slice.

Makes about seven 4-ounce servings

Sumitra's Cheesecake

Sumitra is my Sanskrit name. I invented this for a cheesecake-loving husband who doesn't want a bulging belly.

Crust
12 graham crackers, crushed
6 tablespoons butter, melted

Filling
8 ounces extra-firm or firm tofu
1 pound ricotta cheese
$1/2$ cup Yogurt Cheese (page 51)
$1/2$ cup milk
2 tablespoons tapioca flour or cornstarch
2 teaspoons vanilla extract
$1/2$ cup honey

Vanilla yogurt and sliced soft fruit for topping (optional)

1. To make crust: In a bowl, mix graham cracker crumbs and melted butter. Press into bottom and up sides of a 9-inch pie pan.

2. In a bowl, blend filling ingredients until smooth.

3. Pour into crust. Bake in a preheated at 400°F oven for 40 minutes, or until lightly golden on the edges.

4. If using topping, mix yogurt and fruit, spread on cake, and bake 5 minutes more.

Makes one 9-inch cake; serves 8

Crunchy Chip Cookies

These cookies are not especially low in fat, but they are a highly concentrated food and high in protein. One of these and a green salad keep me going for a long time.

$^1/_4$ cup canola oil
$^1/_2$ cup honey
1 $^1/_4$ cup water
$^1/_2$ cup toasted sunflower seeds
$^1/_2$ cup toasted sesame seeds
1 cup cracked millet
2 cups rolled oats
1 $^1/_2$ cups whole-wheat flour
1 cup chocolate or carob chips

1. In a bowl, mix oil, honey, and water together.

2. Stir in all remaining ingredients. Drop by teaspoonfuls 1-inch apart on oiled baking sheets. Press to flatten into cookie shape.

3. Bake at in a preheated 350°F oven for 20 minutes, or until golden brown.

Makes about 3 dozen cookies

Tunbridge Truffles

This is an infamous snack food that was used to energize work parties erecting a post-and-beam house in Tunbridge, Vermont. This vegetarian pemmican, along with water, can give you energy for the entire day.

> 3 cups dried fruit (apples, apricots, dates, prunes, raisins)
> 1 cup nuts (walnuts, hazelnuts, sunflower seeds, pecans)
> Lemon or orange juice, if needed
> Shredded dried coconut or ground nuts

1. Grind fruit and nuts together in a blender or food processor. Add a little lemon juice or orange juice if it's too dry.

2. Roll into golf-ball-sized balls and roll in coconut or nut meal. (children think that these need a chocolate chip for a surprise middle.)

Makes about 24 truffles

Applesauce Slush

This was discovered by accident but greeted with great enthusiasm: Freeze any amount of applesauce the morning of lunch packing, place it in a plastic thermos or container and by noon — voilà! — slush! It's easier to eat from a straight-sided container. If you freeze it in small yogurt cups, they can be packed into lunches straight from the freezer.

Date-Nut Bars

2 cups dates, pitted
1 cup water
1 teaspoon fresh lemon juice
2 cups rolled oats
1 cup unbleached white or white-wheat flour
$1/_2$ teaspoon salt
1 cup honey
6 tablespoons butter, melted
1 cup chopped walnuts

1. Combine dates and water in a saucepan and simmer until soft and thickened, about 10 minutes (if they don't melt into a thick puree, puree in a blender, then cook on low heat a few minutes more). Stir in lemon juice. Set aside.

2. Grind oats to a gritty flour in a blender. In a bowl, mix with flour, salt, and honey. Stir in melted butter to moisten all dry ingredients.

3. Press half of oat mixture into a buttered 8- x 8-inch baking dish.

4. Spread on filling, then crumble the rest of the oat mixture on top (I use a cheese grater to get an even crumble). Sprinkle with walnuts. Bake in a preheated 350°F for 30 minutes, or until golden brown. Let cool, then cut into squares.

Makes 9 bars

Soy Prisms

These can be eaten as is, or served with Rainbow Prisms (page 191).

   2 cups soy milk
   $1/_3$ cup agar agar
   $1/_3$ cup maple syrup
   4 tablespoons soy flour

1. In a dry heavy skillet, toast soy flour on medium-low heat for about 10 to 15 minutes, or until golden and fragrant.

2. In a saucepan, mix soy milk and agar agar together. Cook over medium heat until mixture begins to thicken, about 10 minutes.

3. Stir in maple syrup and soy flour. Simmer, stirring constantly, until thickened.

4. Pour into a 9- x 12-inch baking dish and smooth. Let cool completely. Cut into small cubes or triangles and lift out with a spatula.

Honey Melon

Chelsea, a fifth-grade student of mine, brought this light and delicious dessert to our Greek feast.

   1 tablespoon pure lemon juice
   3 tablespoons honey
   1 honeydew melon, peeled, seeded, and cubed

Mix the lemon juice and honey together in a bowl. Add melon and stir to coat.

Serves 4

Rainbow Prisms

2 tablespoons fresh lemon juice

I tablespoon honey

I cup diced peaches or mangoes

I cup diced pineapple

I cup halved red grapes

I cup diced honeydew melon

Cashew Cream (page 165)

1. In a bowl, mix honey and lemon juice together. Add remaining ingredients and gently stir to coat.

2. Dribble on a bit of Nut Cream (page 165) just before eating.

Serves 6

Squash Hermits

$1/4$ cup soy flour

I $1/2$ cups whole-wheat flour

I teaspoon baking soda

$1/2$ teaspoon baking powder

$1/2$ teaspoon salt

$1/2$ teaspoon ground cinnamon

$1/2$ teaspoon ground allspice

Pinch of ground nutmeg

6 tablespoons butter at room temperature

I cup winter squash puree

$3/4$ cup molasses

$1/2$ cup chopped walnuts

$^1/_2$ cup sunflower seeds

1 cup dried currants or chopped raisins

1. In separate bowls, combine dry ingredients and wet ingredients.

2. Mix both together. Stir in chopped nuts and fruits.

3. Spread $^1/_2$-inch thick onto an oiled baking sheet. Bake in a preheated 350°F oven for 30 minutes, or until golden. Let cool. Cut into squares or rectangles.

Makes about 18 squares

Sweet Potato Pudding

Nut Cream (page 165) is nice on this.

3 cups milk

2 sweet potatoes, baked, peeled, and mashed

$^1/_4$ cup honey

$^1/_2$ cup cornstarch

Pinch of salt

Pinch of ground nutmeg

1. In a saucepan, mix all ingredients together except nutmeg. Simmer, stirring constantly, until thickened, about 15 minutes.

2. Pour into containers and sprinkle with nutmeg.

Variation: Use 2 cups pureed butternut squash instead of sweet potato, replace honey with $^3/_4$ cup molasses, and add $^1/_4$ teaspoon ground ginger, $^1/_4$ teaspoon ground cinnamon, and $^1/_4$ teaspoon ground cloves.

Serves 6

Indian Pudding

To those of you who don't live in New England or haven't tasted this pudding, I know that it sounds strange. It is really quite delicious and one of my favorite desserts. Well, all right, most gooey chocolate desserts come before it.

This is one of those early colonial recipes (like baked beans). People didn't work on the Sabbath, so Saturday night while the oven was still warm, a pot of beans and a dish of this pudding would be baked in a slowly cooling oven all night. Needless to say, cooking times and temperatures, along with flour coarseness, were variables. My mom made the recipe foolproof by adding the tapioca.

This is a good way to use up a lot of milk that is about to go sour. Nice with Nut Cream (page 165) on top.

$4 \frac{1}{2}$ cups milk
$\frac{3}{4}$ cup cornmeal
3 tablespoons tapioca, grain-sized
$1 \frac{1}{2}$ teaspoons salt
$\frac{1}{2}$ cup honey
1 cup molasses
1 teaspoon ground ginger
$\frac{1}{2}$ teaspoon ground cinnamon
2 tablespoons butter

1. In a saucepan, heat 4 cups of milk until bubbles form around the edges. Remove 1 cup of the scalded milk and set aside.

2. In a bowl, mix cornmeal, remaining $\frac{1}{2}$ cup milk, and tapioca and add to pan of hot milk. Simmer for 20 minutes, stirring frequently.

3. Stir in all remaining ingredients except 1 cup scalded milk.

4. Pour all into a buttered 5-cup baking dish.

5. Pour remaining I cup milk over top. Bake for 3 hours in a preheated 250° to 300°F oven. Let cool until set.

Serves 6

Pumpkin or Squash Pie

3 cups mashed pumpkin or squash
2 to 3 tablespoons cornstarch
$1/2$ teaspoon ground cinnamon
$1/2$ teaspoon ground ginger
$1/4$ teaspoon ground nutmeg
$1/2$ teaspoon salt
$1/4$ teaspoon ground cloves
2 tablespoons butter
I cup milk or Nut Milk (page 162)
$1/2$ cup molasses
$1/2$ cup honey
9-inch pie crust

1. Combine all ingredients except crust in a saucepan and stir until smooth. Cook over low heat until thickened, about 10 to 15 minutes.

2. Pour into unbaked pie crust. Bake in a preheated 425°F oven for 15 minutes. Reduce heat to 350°F and bake 20 to 30 minutes longer, or until set and crust is golden.

Makes one 9-inch pie; serves 6

Stuffed Dates

Pitted dates
Yogurt Cheese (page 51) or raw almonds
Ground walnuts or shredded dried coconut

1. Slit top of dates lengthwise and remove pits.

2. Fill cavity with yogurt cheese or an almond. Roll in walnuts or coconut.

Sesame Pudding

$1/2$ cup tahini
$1/2$ cup arrowroot, cornstarch, or tapioca flour
$1/2$ cup honey or barley malt
4 cups water
1 teaspoon ground ginger
2 cups mixed walnuts, coconut, and finely diced dried fruit

1. In a saucepan, stir together all ingredients except nuts, coconut, and dried fruit. Heat over low heat, stirring until thickened, about 15 minutes.

2. Fold in nuts, dried fruit, and coconut. Refrigerate for about 2 hours, or until set.

Serves 6

Rice Pudding

This is good cold or warm in a thermos; it tastes good topped with Nut Cream (page 165).

$^3/_4$ cup water
1 cup brown rice
Pinch of salt
$^1/_4$ cup raisins
2 cups milk
Pinch of ground cardamom
$^1/_2$ teaspoon ground coriander
$^1/_2$ cup shredded dried coconut
$^1/_2$ cup honey

1. In a saucepan, bring water to a boil. Add rice, reduce heat to low, cover, and cook for 20 minutes, or until water is absorbed. Rice will be only half cooked.

2. Stir in salt, raisins, milk, cardamom, and coriander. Cover and simmer for 20 to 30 minutes.

3. Add coconut and honey. Let sit for 15 minutes.

Serves 4

Cheese-Fruit Mousse

I peach, peeled and pitted
I apple, peeled and cored
I banana, peeled
$1/2$ cup chopped pineapple
I orange, peeled
I to $1 1/2$ cups apple or orange juice, as needed
$1/2$ cup quartered grapes
$1/2$ cup arrowroot
$1/2$ cup ricotta cheese
$1/2$ cup plain yogurt
$3/4$ cup shredded Cheddar cheese
Pinch of ground nutmeg

1. Chop fruit, saving juices.

2. Add apple or orange juice to reserved juices to make $1 1/2$ cups. In a saucepan, whisk arrowroot into juice. Simmer until thickened, about 5 to 10 minutes.

3. Remove from heat. Stir in ricotta cheese and yogurt, then fruit and cheese.

4. Refrigerate for at least 2 to 3 hours. Serve sprinkled with nutmeg.

Serves 6

Index

New World Library is dedicated to
publishing books, audio cassettes, and videotapes that inspire
and challenge us to improve the quality
of our lives and our world.

Our books and tapes are available
in bookstores everywhere.
For a catalog of our complete library
of fine books and cassettes, contact:

New World Library
14 Pamaron Way
Novato, CA 94949

Telephone: (415) 884-2100
Fax: (415) 884-2199
Or call toll-free (800) 972-6657
Catalog requests: Ext. 50
Ordering: Ext. 52

E-mail: escort@nwlib.com
http://www.nwlib.com